BOOKSE

Deborah Elliott,
Philip Grey
&
Ian Miller

TEACH YOURSELF BOOKS
Hodder and Stoughton

The authors and publishers are grateful to the Sevenoaks Bookshop for the use of their facilities for the cover photograph.

First published 1990
Copyright © 1990
Deborah Elliott, Philip Grey & Ian Miller

No part of this publication may be reproduced or transmitted in any form or by any means, electronically or mechanically, including photocopying, recording or any information storage or retrieval system, without either the prior permission in writing from the publisher or a licence, permitting restricted copying, issued by the Copyright Licensing Agency, 33–34 Alfred Place, London WC1E 7DP

ISBN 0 340 42876 7

Phototypeset by Input Typesetting Ltd, London
Printed and bound in Great Britain
for Hodder and Stoughton Educational
a division of Hodder and Stoughton Ltd,
Mill Road, Dunton Green, Sevenoaks, Kent,
by Richard Clay Ltd, Bungay, Suffolk

Contents

Foreword v

Introduction vi

1 **Daily Routine** 1
Business is simple . . . The basic model. Starting the day. Orders! The morning mail. *The Bookseller*. Daily tasks. There's always a customer. Training new staff. Invoices, payments and banking. Back to the customer. Watching the business. Deliveries. 'Net' books. 'Non-net' books. Buying new books. The customer again. The end of the day.

2 **Ordering** 16
Book evaluation. Special arrangements. Order forms. Teleordering. Small orders. BA Giro ordering scheme. Ordering from overseas. Distribution. Unavailable titles. Stock ordering.

3 **Stock Control** 34
Stock cards. Computer stock control. Ordering for seasonal peaks. Bargain books.

4 **Bookshop Accounting** 43
Management accounts. Margins. Shrinkage. Stocktaking. Ledgers. Methods of payments. Incoming invoices. Returns. Expenses. Bank overdraft and loans. Computerisation. Credit arrangements and cash flow.

5 **Setting Up a Bookshop** 58
The type and style of shop. Market research. Creating a budget. Engaging an accountant and a solicitor. Locating a retail site. Seeking finance. Negotiating with the landlord. Fitting out. Staff. Countdown to opening. Stock. Franchising.

6 Marketing and Promotion 93
What is marketing? What about advertising, and reputation? How does this affect bookselling? Promotion.

7 Bibliography 108
Introduction. Whitaker's sources. British National Bibliography (BNB). CIP data. Books in English (BIE). BLAISE-LINE. Book Data. USA bibliographies. Publishers' catalogues. Other sources.

8 Introducing Technology 127
Bookshop systems. Electronic communications networks. Information technology. The future?

9 Law for Booksellers 131
The Net Book Agreement. Law of copyright. The Obscene Publications Act. Law for retailers.

10 The Trade Organisations 144
The Booksellers Association. The Publishers Association. Book Trust. Book House Training Centre. The Library Association. The Society of Young Publishers. The Society of Authors. The Independent Publishers Guild. The Book Publishers Representatives Association. The International Booksellers Federation.

Appendix 1 Annual Book Trade Events 157
Appendix 2 Book Trade Journals 159
Appendix 3 Book Trade Organisation Addresses 162
Appendix 4 Book Tokens Ltd, Rules and Instructions 166
Appendix 5 Net Book Agreement 1957 171
Appendix 6 Library Licence 173
Appendix 7 The Book Agent's Licence 176
Appendix 8 Quantity Book Buying Licence 178
Appendix 9 Primary and Secondary School Licence 181
Appendix 10 Services Unit Libraries Licence 183

Foreword

To enter the world of bookselling today is to become part of an increasingly professional and competitive trade. While an affinity with books and the printed word may be one of the reasons for considering working in a bookshop, the successful bookseller will need both to understand fully today's sophisticated retail book trade, and to develop a broad range of skills.

Teach Yourself Bookselling is an excellent introduction to bookselling, and the Booksellers Association welcomes this addition to current information on the trade. Furthermore, we are pleased to be involved with the publishers, Hodder & Stoughton, who generously sponsor the annual *Teach Yourself Books Award* for the most successful student completing the BA's Training Qualification, 'The Certificate in Bookselling Skills'.

Finally, the BA will, of course, be happy to help with any queries on bookselling from readers.

Tim Godfray
Director

Deborah Elliott started her career at Foyles in 1978. She has worked for a number of major bookselling companies, and was for 3 years the Trade Practice Executive of the Booksellers Association. Her involvement with training began in 1983 following her success as BA Charter Student of the Year, and she has since helped to set up and tutor the BA CIBS qualification. She has also lectured abroad, and currently works for Book Data.

Philip Grey is Director of Retail Services at Warwick University, and has been in academic and general bookselling all his working life, beginning in London's Charing Cross Road in 1960. He has lectured extensively for the BA, and independently for university and high street booksellers both in the UK and overseas.

Ian Miller entered the book trade in 1949, working for Mowbrays in Birmingham and London for 15 years. He then became personnel and training manager for Hudsons Bookshops until 1981, when he set up his own management and training consultancy. He was for many years actively involved with the development of BA training, and now works independently for several major bookselling companies.

Introduction

Not gods, nor men, nor even booksellers have put up with poets being second-rate.

For those about to enter the world of bookselling, it may be of interest to note what the poet Horace thought about the trade in the first century BC. He seems to have credited booksellers with certain standards, doubtless influenced by sound commercial principles: whereas gods and men may reject the second-rate poet for aesthetic reasons, the canny bookseller spurns him as a non-saleable commodity.

This perhaps illustrates the main purpose of our book: to point out that bookselling, however romantic its appeal, is a retail business whose primary function is to make a profit.

For many years, the classic image of a bookshop has been of a quaint old shop piled high with dusty volumes, run by an eccentric but knowledgeable book-lover. To mention sales and profits was almost considered bad taste. Over the last decade, however, the bookselling scene has changed dramatically.

Most will have heard of the retail revolution – more people with more money on the High Streets and, as a result, more retailers competing to profit from the high disposable incomes. Retailing has had to become more professional, prompted by the consumer who has become more critically aware of where he spends his money, and on what. Retailers are now jockeying for prime positions on the High Street, are investing more in store design and market research, and are applying to their businesses managerial and financial principles previously only found in industry.

Today's large, successful bookselling companies are those who were in the forefront of these changes in retailing and, most importantly, who understood that they were no longer only in competition with other booksellers, but also with everyone else on the High Street for the pound in the consumer's pocket – the so-called 'leisure pound'.

In many ways, this is one of the most exciting times to be a part of the bookselling trade. Any revolution brings opportunities, but conversely the challenges facing today's bookseller are also great: competition in the High Street, the threat of abolition of resale price maintenance, the single European market and the possible imposition of VAT on books might all pose very real problems to anyone hoping to start an independent business in the 90's.

In order to compete with the chains (most of whom have a presence in every major town today), many booksellers have successfully taken up 'niche' bookselling, otherwise known as specialisation. The chains try to cover a very wide range of subjects, and although many of them do an excellent job, it would be unrealistic for anyone to expect to meet all the needs of the special-interest sectors of the book-buying public. This is where the perceptive independent bookseller can profitably step in.

The horizons of the bookselling world have widened dramatically in the past few years. Not only has our view shifted from the quiet country village shop to the bustling commerce of the inner city megastore, but we now have to look to Westminster and Brussels for changes in legislation affecting the trade. With the coming of the single European market, influences from across the channel will come into play, and competition will become even fiercer.

The publishing industry is ahead of its retailing cousin in experiencing this. Always more international in its trading, with foreign rights sales and overseas publishing divisions, it has been the subject of so many buy-outs and mergers in recent years that booksellers now find it hard to know where to place their orders from week to week. In the face of mergers in bookselling, the independent bookshop has a hard job maintaining a clear personal identity in the market-place, and must be prepared to invest in strong marketing and promotional strategies.

With all these forces in play, and around 50 000 new books per year to choose from, today's bookseller is a very different proposition from the picture we have drawn of his absent-minded, bibliophile ancestor. To keep up with his competitors and to prosper, he must be part financial whizz-kid, part one-minute manager, part political visionary, and must also possess the instinct to handle and sell books well.

It's a great challenge, but then we believe it's a great trade. In spite of today's pressures, books still have not become just another commodity. The retailing principles may be the same, but for most of us selling books is not like selling tins of baked beans, and the claim made back in 1962 at the NBA hearing that 'books are different' thankfully still holds true.

This book is intended for everyone new to bookselling, whether you are just starting as a sales assistant in a branch of one of the large chains, or contemplating buying and running your own business. Although written from the viewpoint of the bookshop owner, everything in the book is relevant to the ambitious employee in an established High Street store or the experienced sales assistant who is thinking of going it alone. Throughout, the bookshop owner is referred to as 'he'. We would like to stress that this is purely for the sake of convenience and that any apparent discrimination is unintentional.

We hope that *Teach Yourself Bookselling* whets your appetite, and wish you a long, happy, and above all, prosperous career in what we believe to be the most rewarding of trades.

Deborah Elliott
Philip Grey
Ian Miller

1

Daily Routine

Business is simple . . .

The daily routine of running a bookshop is much the same as running any retail shop, selling any range of products. The principle of selling books for a profit, in order to pay the rent, staff wages and the basic expenses of day-to-day needs and services, with the aim of making a net gain at the end of the trading year, is a simple routine in itself. But whoever first said, 'Business is simple' was taking for granted the two important ingredients of starting – and continuing – in business: hard work and attention to detail, which make the simple routine run effectively.

Bookselling is no exception, and has its own trade protocol, methods and peculiarities to be taken into account.

Books carry an air of intellectual glamour, mystery, learning and pleasure which many people can appreciate and enjoy in the abstract, but applying commercial acumen to the stocking and selling of books by the hundred or thousand can soon diminish that sense of glamour. Before going into the details of bookselling as a trade, it's worth looking at the tasks a bookshop owner needs to do in a typical day.

The Basic Model

To keep the examples in this book to a recognisable scale, we'll assume that the shop employs five people, one of whom is the owner, who works every day of the week. The annual income – turnover – of the business is £250 000, or just under £5000 per week. Anyone intending to start in bookselling should not consider a turnover below this figure, since it is the minimum level at which a reasonable living might be gained by an owner. Further, as we shall see, a shop must grow to survive, and too small a start will dictate many factors which may inhibit that vital growth.

Starting the Day

The owner will arrive some time before the usual opening time of 9 o'clock, to unlock any internal doors, open the safe and prepare a change float for the till, and to sort out any principal jobs for his staff. The shop assistants will arrive a few minutes before opening time, and may have their own set routines for the day, depending on the time of the week. Presuming that the shop trades six days per week, but the staff work for only five, then of the five employees, there will only be three besides the owner because one person will be having a day off. The busiest day will probably be Saturday, when a Saturday-only assistant will be working. Only by having two staff off on the same day can the manager ensure that one especially busy day is fully staffed.

The shop will need tidying from the day before, especially if today is a Monday: Saturday business is usually heavier than during the week, and displays and sections will have been moved around and depleted. It may be that the window display needs changing, in preparation for new titles being released during the week. This tidying work needs doing first thing, so that the shop looks attractive for the next likely busy time over lunch.

Orders!

The stock control system (manual or computerised) should be checked to see what books need to be re-ordered, and there will be decisions to be made about how many. Saturdays bring a lot of enquiries and orders for titles which aren't normally in stock, so these orders must be prepared, despatched and filed. These jobs need to be done early in the day, when the shop is likely to be quiet; there may not be time from mid-day onwards, and the new day's trade will bring more orders and fresh jobs.

The Morning Mail

The mail will be sorted by the owner, and will include catalogues, invoices, orders, letters from suppliers and customers, and statements of account if it is the start of the month. Post on a Monday is heavier because second-class mail from the end of the previous week will have been cleared over the weekend. The owner will deal with the accounts correspondence, but after looking through the day's orders to see what business is being done, he will pass these to an assistant who will check if they are in stock; for speed, the stock control system may be checked first.

A manual card system will show if the book is normally kept in stock, and if it is, the shelves are checked for copies. If it isn't normally in stock, it can be added to the pile of special orders which have accumulated over the weekend. If it is on the shelf then the customer can be advised by phone or postcard, or the book can be sent by post with an invoice or a credit card slip. The book may normally be in stock, but has sold out for the moment – any outstanding orders for such stock are then annotated to show that a special order is waiting.

If the stock control system is computerised (systems are discussed elsewhere in this book) then maybe all of these processes can be handled through the computer terminal. But there is no substitute for checking the stock shelves anyway, to make sure.

Some of these orders may need checking, to ensure that the details are correct: there are well over 560 000 British books in print at any one time, and more than 61 000 new titles are added each year. More often than not, the customer will want a title which is not available in the shop. These orders need checking in the trade bibliographies before the order is placed. Incorrect author with correct title, or vice versa, accepting the customer's publisher details without checking, or not realising that there is a paperback and cheaper edition available, can cause enough confusion to delay the order unnecessarily, or bring the wrong book altogether.

If a shop has a healthy level of incoming orders, then they should be logged in a receiving book, showing the date received, the customer's name, any order reference, and details of any cheques enclosed with the order. Many shops will estimate the value of the order so that a continuing order book value can be assessed, and used in the future budgeting of this side of the business. This log book will also indicate if there is a growing custom with particular clients.

Daily Tasks

Elsewhere staff will be cleaning the shop area, tidying the office or behind the scenes. The shop diary may show that a publisher's representative is due, and the owner may want to check his stock records in time to place orders for more copies, as well as the new titles that will be shown. Publishers' sales representatives are probably the most frequent trade visitors to bookshops, and the manager will want to see their lists of books to be published in the near future.

There's Always a Customer

Early mornings may be quiet, but there will always be someone in the shop, browsing or enquiring about a new title or an order placed some time before. The phone will need answering, and it will not be long before the mid-morning post brings the first parcels of the day, as well as possibly more orders and correspondence. To keep the shelves stocked and customer orders satisfied, the incoming parcels need checking and the books pricing and shelving, as regularly as possible. Between early lunchtime and late afternoon there may be several more deliveries from the various carriers who call.

Training New Staff

In a well-planned routine, most of the staff will know what to do; but a new member of staff may have recently started, and his or her work will need to be checked and new jobs arranged. The owner will probably do much of this himself, though he may pass the newcomer on to an experienced member of staff who will oversee the trainee's practice. Such training is essential in any business, but never more so than in a small concern where an additional member of staff will eventually undertake a substantial part of the work. If the training is insufficient or inadequate, new staff will both feel and be inefficient; more especially, the business will suffer because mistakes may be made which lose business.

The risk inherent in taking on and training new staff often leads owners of small businesses to do all the training themselves, on the 'do as I do' or 'sitting by Nellie' basis. It is far better to plan beforehand what a new person will have to do, and then split the training work between several staff members. This means that the new person learns the various jobs from the people who actually do them daily, and gets to know all the staff quickly. The owner may claim to know what is done, but not actually do the tasks as regularly as his staff.

This induction training should be programmed at a reasonable pace, written out in a timetabled approach, and spread over several days, allowing for both training and practice by the new staff. Everyone will then know who will be training what and when, and no one person's time will be monopolised by a new member of staff who will need attention and patience. Everyone, including the owner, will be free to continue the ordinary day's work at some stage, and will not get behind.

Training is of increasing importance as High Street and European competition grows; even small companies need to consider what external training may be available for their staff. Though it may be awkward to release staff for day courses, the benefits are well worth the effort and the cost. In addition to meeting other trainees in an independent environment, training is more formalised, and takes into account good practice which the trainee will bring back to the benefit of the company.

Such training should not of course be restricted to the new member of staff; everyone will need re-training or skill reinforcement from time to time, including the owner. Past training in any aspect of business is no guarantee of present excellence, and more than likely the older the member of staff, the more need there is for entrenched views and even bad habits to be reassessed and brought up to date.

Certificate in Bookselling Skills (CIBS)

The Certificate in Bookselling Skills is a Booksellers Association package providing in-shop training aids which can be used for the induction of new recruits with no previous bookselling or retailing experience. It covers all aspects of training staff as they progress through the range of duties and responsibilities they will meet as their experience grows.

The initial package has an Induction Guide, outlining the basic elements of starting a job; a Study Guide, including a tape, which outlines the CIBS system and the way study and assessment is carried out; and a starter manual – Level 1 – which introduces shop work, the customer, money procedures, stock and the work premises. Manual 2 is divided into two parts: the first covers the book itself, bibliographic skills and trade practice, the second deals with stock knowledge and book evaluation, finance, marketing and management.

The package as a whole works on the open-learning basis, so that the student progresses at his or her own learning pace. Someone in the shop acts as a shop trainer – probably the owner in the case of our model shop – and for Level 2 students there is an externally appointed tutor who can provide help and advice, and marks the assignments which are set in these later packages.

The end result is a nationally recognised certificate specific to bookselling, but which is also closely allied to the basic training in a wide range of retail outlets. The Certificate is, in that sense, expected to be 'portable' and of use beyond bookselling should the student choose another retail trade.

At the time of writing (1990), the first package costs £60 and the second (Level 2 is in two sections) is £110. Together they represent a thorough and professional approach to training at all levels. For the small and busy bookshop, not only are the results of good training likely to be effective in a very direct way, but much time is saved for the owner, who must otherwise plan and detail staff training for himself.

Invoices, Payments and Banking

The mail may have brought payments of invoices issued by the shop, and invoices sent by suppliers for books despatched separately. New orders from customers may mean that a typist needs to prepare the paperwork for deliveries of books from stock to a local school or company. It will be best to file the incoming invoices and statements until the regular day set aside for clearing accounting matters, but payments coming in will need to be banked. If Saturday's takings were not counted and banked in the night-safe over the weekend, then the money must be counted now and taken to the bank along with any payments received in the morning post. This work must be accurately done in a secure office, and can take up quite a bit of time – Friday's takings may not have been counted if Saturday is a busy trading day, so both days' takings must be separately counted. If the money does not balance with the till reading, the discrepancy must be traced; cheques need to be quickly looked over for any simple errors. Was the right credit card used on the right voucher? And so on . . .

Back to the Customer . . .

Morning coffee, lunch and the afternoon break will mean only half the staff on the shop floor for the hour and a half involved, and with background routines going on all the time, it could be easy to overlook the customers. Not all ask for what they want, not all can find what they want, and a good many will not know what they want. 40% will buy on impulse, and 60% will leave without buying anything at all. During the week, 60% will be women out shopping. They may be buying small books for their young children, or presents for others. Books are widely advertised in the media, often indirectly: a TV serial may mean enquiries for a famous book, a film at the local cinema may create a demand just for that week. The weekend papers will have reviewed at least 20 or 30 new titles due shortly, or published the week before. There may be a fiction serial on the radio, or the fifth part of a cookery course on the TV. Political events may spur interest in a biography, or the death of someone famous will create a demand for their books or books about them. Adverts in the Sunday papers will create interest but not always orders. And of course the season will bring its own pressures – Easter, Christmas, summer holidays will all create different reading needs. In spite of all this exposure, it is estimated that up to 50% of the population who could read books, don't.

Watching the Business

Apart from routine accounting, a retail business, like any other, needs to plan its development, in part by keeping track of what is already happening to its daily trade. Good or disappointing sales over a period need to be reviewed so that highs can be built on, or falling sales trends corrected. So where sales are showing higher peaks in certain weeks or seasons, relevant stock can be bought to maximise such sales, and a note can be made for subsequent years that, say, Easter was surprisingly good. On the other hand, sales may be much lower than expected in, say, the September back-to-college period. This will mean that stock should be reduced for such periods, unless a reason can be found to explain why sales were disappointing – are the college students sufficiently aware of the shop, do the lecturers know that the shop stocks college textbooks? If the answer is simply that the shop is too far away for students to visit and buy, then money tied up in textbooks should be directed towards other types of books and subjects.

Beware of sudden highs or lows in trading – they may be a freak of weather or local events, and may not last. A trend is a longer term difference in trading volume or purchase types, and may need investigation.

A new business will have presented budgets and plans for cash requirements to the bank manager, and these need checking as time goes on. Past sales will indicate how much cash is needed, or is available for new purchases. Without constant review, the business can change course and perhaps get into difficulties. So the manager will probably keep a daily chart of expected sales, which incidentally encourages staff to take an interest in how the shop is doing.

Invoiced sales can change a great deal from one month to another, depending on the type of customer, and here again trends could mean budget reviews. So each day the owner should look at the latest figures and compare them to expectations. The bank overdraft will need to be reviewed every so often with the bank manager, and he will expect to be given an idea of future sales so that he can help assess the cash needs of the business.

Although a great deal of time need not be spent each day on this kind of planning, keeping an eye on the shop's progress is an essential part of the daily routine.

Deliveries

Deliveries will need unpacking, checking and the books shelving for sale as soon as possible. Each invoice will show the cost price and the selling price of the books received; the margin between the two can vary considerably and needs scrutiny. Special orders may attract small order charges or low discounts, and packing and invoice errors will need correction. In the case of educational or academic stock, quite a few books will need pricing, since prices are not always printed on every book. Some titles again will need higher prices than recommended by the publisher, because the margin is too low to produce a profit, or surcharges may need to be absorbed.

'Net' Books

The majority of books supplied are called net books, because their price is that set by the publisher and they cannot be sold any cheaper (see Chapter 9). There is nothing to prevent an increase in price, however, and in some cases the selling price may need to be higher or the book will be sold at a trading loss.

'Non-net' Books

Some books are supplied at non-net prices, which means that they can be discounted if the shop wishes. These are mainly school books which are sold in bulk as class sets, the idea being that volume sales suggest lower prices to the teacher or school. In fact, such books are usually supplied at half the normal discount margin anyway, 17.5%, and discounting them even further is not sound business unless you are dealing in considerable quantities. Bookshops do not normally stock such titles for these reasons but where they choose to do so, it is common, and legitimate, to increase the price of single copies on the shelf to reflect the usual discount margin of 35%. Some publishers' catalogues state that teachers should anticipate this when visiting a bookshop to view school textbooks.

Buying New Books

Though the actual figures can vary considerably, about 80% of the stock held in a bookshop may be 'back-stock'; this is, titles which have been available for some while. The remaining 20% will be new titles, published each week, and each day of each week. One new title is published every 2 minutes of the working day, throughout the year, and the job of selecting from this huge range – more than 61 000 per annum – could be a daunting one.

Most publishers will have a representative who visits account customers to take orders for new books. This is called 'subscribing', a term dating from the days when books were often published as part-works, as were many of Dickens' novels, for instance.* If the publisher does not have a representative, they may ask a freelance rep to carry their list for them. The model shop we are using could choose to use a wholesaler as principal supplier, in which case the wholesaler may send a rep, or rely on catalogues, *The Bookseller*, wholesalers' lists and adverts to catch up with required titles. Nevertheless most of the paperback companies and the larger general publishers will want to have a rep calling, so that new books get the wide publicity they need.

A paperback company will expect their rep to visit the shop monthly, to show the books which will be available towards the end of the following month. Close to publication date, the buyer should be able to see the jackets of all the planned books, and for important books finished copies are often available too. These jackets, along with the rep's description and the 'blurb' – the write-up on the back or inside of the jacket – provide the basis for a decision on whether or not to buy the book, and in what quantity.

Obviously, the design and presentation of the cover are important – what strikes the buyer as interesting, attractive, powerful or startling will strike the potential customer in the same way. But the jacket is the book's advert, and in many cases will sell a book which has little merit as a good read or a work of literature. The rep will know if the author is expected to be read widely, or will appear on TV, or if the book will be coming out as a film. He may be able to point out local material in the book, or local

*Where the subscriptions before publication helped to finance the cost of production.

authorship, or he may know that the buyer is interested in the subject matter of the book, because the shop specialises in that field.

Price will be an important factor; the average price of paperbacks in *The Bookseller*'s Top Ten is under £5.00. For a book to cost more than this, there should be added features; illustrations, a film or TV tie-in (with a cover picture from the screen) or simply size – a trilogy in one volume, a large format production or just a long book!

The buyer will soon develop a 'nose' for what will and won't sell in his shop, and need not spend time looking at books for which he is unlikely to have a sale – unless the rep is able to point out a special feature which needs taking into account.

No buyer should purchase books which do not provide him with a good trading margin; most paperback companies will give a 35% discount but this could be higher depending on the shop's turnover with a particular publisher. Thus a shop buying a great many paperbacks on a regular basis from a publisher could negotiate a higher discount than a shop buying relatively few paperbacks from that supplier. More discount is available for shops larger than our model, who may well make special efforts to promote certain publishers' titles, and in some cases will set up areas, or shops-within-shops, to highlight a particular series or imprint. Some suppliers will agree a new discount level which appears on the invoice, other will award a retrospective credit when a certain level of sales has been reached.

Nevertheless, the buyer should beware of taking too many of a title, simply because it is supposed to be important. The cost of returning books to suppliers (which is dealt with on p. 52) is high, and cash is tied up in stock whilst the books are being returned and a credit note sent. Wholesalers can give a very quick service, to catch up with those titles which begin to 'run away'. A good many new paperbacks are published in counter-packs of 12, 24 or 20, and in dumpbins (larger, floor-standing display packs) of anything from 24 to 72. These display packs are very useful and attractive, particularly if the buyer has committed himself to a large order, but should not be a temptation to raise a larger order than is really likely to sell.

The general publisher's rep is more likely to call every three months, taking orders for books publishing up to that time ahead.

Consequently he has less information about some of his titles, and he is unlikely to carry finished copies, unless a really important book is on the way. Here the job of both selling and buying is more difficult, because the range of available subjects and authors is much wider than with the paperback companies, who produce a high level of new fiction. With non-fiction books there is a much greater need to see what the text is like, what the illustrations will be, and generally to know more about the 'feel' of the book.

Dustjackets were originally produced to do just that – protect the binding from dust and scuffs. They have long been used as the travelling advert for the book, and the rep should have a dustcover for every title he wants to show. If he doesn't have one, he will have an editorial page of blurb giving the main details of the book, which could be a rush publication because of some recent political or legal development.

With either paperback or hardback, the established author and his track record are the best guidelines to the book buyer; even here, caution is needed because hardback fiction is notoriously difficult to sell at the average price of £11.00 or so a volume. Although this price compares well in the general arena of arts and leisure interests – compact disc, theatre, concert, a restaurant meal – the general public see such books as expensive, even though they can be read and re-read, and many appreciate in value as first editions by a collected author.*

The difficulty of selling such books – and many illustrated non-fiction books fall into this category as well – is not just the fact that a paperback edition will be available within a few months (though sometimes simultaneously). The public library system means that almost every community has a wide range of freely available books and, without the sense of book ownership, many readers see no need at all to go into a bookshop, or to buy a book. Since, therefore, many books will be bought as gifts rather than as personal copies, the publication of many titles is geared

*A 'first edition' is the true first printing of a book when it is first published. The reverse of a book's title page will indicate this, e.g. 'First published in 1988'; if this is followed by 'reprinted 1988' or 'Second impression 1988', then the book is *not* a first edition.

in this direction, and timed to be available for the main gift seasons, especially at Christmas of course.

A good book therefore needs *selling;* it should have a good cover, a well-known or at least authoritative author, a reasonable price, good illustrations – which may involve line-drawings, black and white and/or colour photographs – and the book should have an acceptable authority in its field. A new travel book about the Lake District of England, for example, must have all these qualities and more if it is to stand up to all the previous very good titles published about the area. There may be the additional need, as with the Lake District example, for the book to appear at the right time of year – either in the spring or early summer for use during the holiday/walking season, or towards Christmas if the book is a pictorial gift volume.

The rep and his company should be able to help here, with display material in the form of posters or display cards. There may be a considerable advertising programme arranged for the book, with signing sessions by the author, newspaper adverts and special reviews in popular magazines and periodicals. To take advantage of these features, the buyer needs to give the book a high level of display in the window, and a high profile in the shop itself. If he is buying a very popular book in quantity, then he will be competing with other bookshops in the town or area, and the chain shops will lose no time in putting their own muscle behind the big titles.

All these points are taken into account when buying new books, and in the background all the time is the need to check buying margins. Whilst paperback companies will have one buying discount for that particular shop, the more general publisher may have several levels of buying discount. If the book is important, then it should carry at least a 35% margin. Thankfully, the days are receding when books were priced according to the perceived market, and it was the bookseller who bore the reduction in margin, simply so that the price could be held. But this practice is still widespread on many lesser titles which may be important to the specialist buyer. Margins as low as 25% and 30% are commonplace on academic and specialist publications. This is a reflection of the fact that the publisher will create the demand for an academic title, for example by getting a textbook adopted for a particular course, thereby generating an order for 30 or 40 copies in the local bookshop. Hence, these titles carry less discount owing to the reduced risk involved for the bookseller.

The representative is a key figure in the business of selling and buying; many booksellers today feel they are wasting valuable time seeing a rep – a subscription session can easily take an hour, and several callers in a week can be very disruptive. But getting accurate information and seeing finished jackets and books is essential to the process of keeping a shop up-to-date, and simply not missing important books. A good rep will give constructive help with purchasing, with genuine advice about over- and under-ordering, what the competition is doing, and with the inevitable occasional return of overstocks problem. He should be able to clear up practical details to do with supply, invoicing, display material and such matters as setting up author signing sessions. The regular rep should know his customers well enough to be able to concentrate on what sells in that shop and area, and need not waste time on the irrelevant. He should never over-promote titles, but at the same time needs to hold out for the best order he believes possible for that shop. The whole process of buying needs a great deal more attention than is often given to it; the session should be in an office, not on the shop floor where there can be interruptions, and cold calls – reps calling without appointments (or late!) – should not be tolerated.

The Customer Again

Throughout the daily routine which makes up the job of being a retail bookseller there is the simple, demanding and ever-present need to serve the customer, by helping in the choice of books, or advising on the details of a title to be specially ordered, or simply taking payment at the till. In the background, there is the further service the shop needs to offer – keeping the shop presentation at its best, changing displays, choosing new titles from the supplier, ensuring that staff promote a sense of welcome and service, planning and making visits to outside customers, and providing a fresh appearance in a shop which will see many frequent and regular customers. It is easy to become complacent in a busy shop, and despondent in a quiet one; the cost of success is the constant awareness of how the customer sees the shop when he or she comes through the door, at any time of the day.

The End of the Day

The routines later in the day should not only finish that day's jobs, but should make ready those for the next morning as well. The overnight orders, sent by post or Teleordering (see p. 24), should be ready, letters stamped for posting. Displays and sections should be tidied where needed, or cleared for fresh displays first thing the next day. The window should be checked to see that nothing has fallen, that all books are in position and, if window lights are used, that the timer is ready to turn them off later in the evening.

The diary should be checked to see that everything planned has been done, or needs to be re-planned because there wasn't time. Tomorrow may be an easy day, it may be an awkward one – fewer staff or a lot of reps.

For the owner, this may simply be the start of the rest of the day: accounting work, VAT records, salary preparation, checking bank overdrafts may all have had to be delayed. In fact, it's no time to do such important work, when one is tired and needs a break from routine, but it is so often the case with small businesses. A computer system which can be operated during the day can eliminate such drudgery, but even this needs planning in order to operate effectively. The best contribution the owner or manager can make to the running of the business is to plan the tasks that he and his staff have to do, so that the ones they enjoy doing, that maintain the job as the one they chose in the first place, can be expanded to the maximum. Buying, display, stock control and above all selling should be the main feature of any working day in a bookshop.

2

Ordering

'Ordering' covers those procedures used by the bookseller to obtain supplies of books from the publisher or wholesaler.

Deciding on the quantity to be ordered is a key function of the buyer based on experience, knowledge of the market and any financial constraints; the mechanics are essentially clerical in nature. Well designed systems, whether manual or computerised, determine the overall effectiveness of the bookshop.

There are four main types of orders that need to be placed. *Subscription orders* are those placed with the rep (the publisher's representative) and this term always covers the ordering of new books yet to be published. This is a key part of the buying procedure. Although this type of order is usually placed verbally, it is advisable to give a written confirmation for the bookshop's records. *Stock orders* are those that regularly go through, usually direct to the publisher, topping up the stock and replacing the books sold. The third type of order covers customers' *special orders;* those orders for books that are not stocked, or are out of stock, but which a customer requires. Finally there are *standing orders* for annual publications, or volumes in a series, to be supplied as published over a period of time. In many instances, the publisher's rep will subscribe these anyway, so this type of order is less commonly placed these days, but it does apply to many annual publications.

Each type of order will originate from a different source; the subscription order is placed after examining the actual book, if this is possible. What is normal practice in London may happen less frequently in the provinces, where the subscriptions will be based on the rep's information about the book, rather than an inspection of the *actual* book. Whether you see the book or not will depend on the size of the publisher's programme of new titles, how advanced production is and the number of times the rep can call, apart from the weight problem for reps having to carry finished copies.

Usually a dustjacket is available with the publisher's additional sales information: as part of his preparation for subscribing, the good buyer will have studied the publisher's catalogue and formulated questions to gain more information about each title before taking a decision to buy. There are many factors to consider when subscribing. Experience as well as flair is important, as is the ability to be objective about the market the bookshop serves and the extent of people's disposable income, apart from the subject matter of the book and its price.

As you will be taking a decision about the potential sales of a book that will not be published for some months, a general awareness of political, economic and social trends all have a bearing on the final decision. How a previous book by the same author sold is a factor, but not necessarily the determining one, in the 'risks decision'. Each book must be judged objectively on its merits within any financial constraints imposed on the buyer; the investment in stock is always heavy in bookshops, and you should always be conscious of the need to buy and sell profitably.

Book Evaluation

Experienced booksellers can pick up a book and evaluate it quickly at a subconscious level, taking into account a wide range of questions that run through their minds as the book is handled.

Evaluation falls into four main categories – technical, textual, cultural and market. We will examine each in more detail.

Technical Evaluation

The diagram shows the terminology used when evaluating the external appearance of a book. The dustwrapper or dustjacket will be placed around the cover of a hardback book, so a brief examination of the actual cover material is also advised. The lettering of the title and the author's name and the cover design should give an indication about the subject matter of the book,

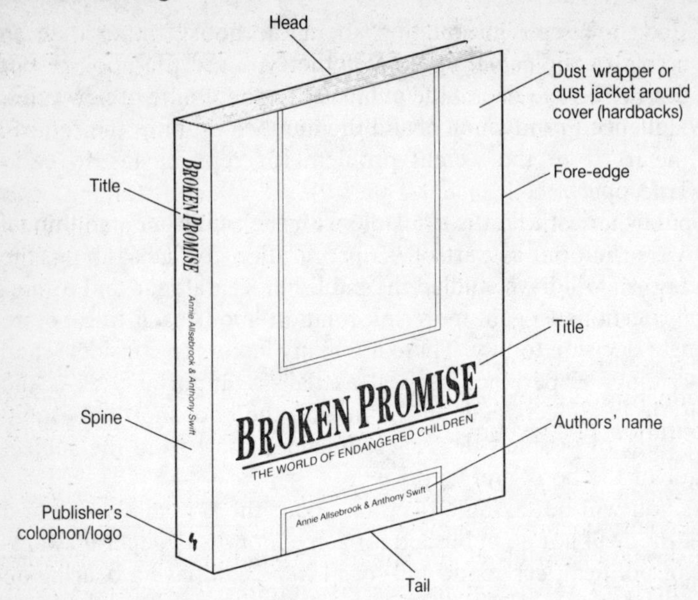

Fig. 1 The technical evaluation of a book.

but may be misleading or unrelated to the content. The design will attempt to sell the book, having visual appeal, especially if placed in a face-on position on the shelf. The fold that tucks under the front cover will show the publisher's 'blurb', being a description of the book; the price will also be shown here. The tuck at the back may continue the text of the blurb, or may give biographical details of the author. On textbooks and paperbacks the blurb will appear on the back cover.

Some books will include a 'headband' to which ribbon markers will be attached, especially in atlases, some reference books and bibles.

The book may also have a coloured 'head', and the head, fore-edge and tail will often be gold-leafed if the book has a special binding; this especially applies to leatherbound books, including bibles.

When you examine the inside of the book, starting with the front and working to the back, you will find the following, common to all books, in the order described. These are known as 'prelims' (preliminaries) and are distinguished by small Latin numerals for the pagination.

a) End papers are located at the front and back; these serve to hold the book to the cover and are usually white paper but can be highly decorated. A single blank page will precede the
b) Half title page which gives the title only; there then follows the
c) Title page which includes the title, the name of author and publisher; on the reverse side of the title page you will find
d) Verso of title page which gives fuller details of the publisher, copyright, Cataloguing in Publication data, ISBN and conditions of sale.

The prelims may also include, as appropriate, a foreword and/or introduction, acknowledgements to those who have helped in the preparation of the book, a table of contents and a list of illustrations.

At the back of the book you may find, depending on the subject matter, an appendix or appendices, a bibliography and an index. You should briefly check the value of these, but at least be aware that the book does contain such information. Assess the size of the book for display in the shop. Look at the quality of the paper and the print used – does the appearance of the page make for easy reading or is it a solid mass of print? Are the illustrations good and the colour satisfactory? Are they located opposite the appropriate text or bound together into the centre of the book? Check the accuracy of the captions to the illustrations, especially references to page numbers, and that the caption actually describes what is shown, e.g. in a railway book the caption describes locomotive no. 5625 where it is clearly 5825. Such errors will not help the sale, especially to a specialist market.

Textual Evaluation

Under this heading you should be considering the subject matter of the book. Ask yourself, is this indicated by the title or is the title misleading? For example, some years ago a book of poetry was published called *The Owl's Nest* which caused much confusion. Is the book a general or specialist view of the subject? What is the scope of the book and the readership level? You need also to consider the authority of the book; by this we mean the reputation of the author and the publisher. What is the basis of the book? Is it original research or based on the work of others? Is it factual or theoretical? Does the author approach the subject objectively or subjectively? Not all these points are relevant to all books, but they indicate the approach you should adopt when evaluating a book so that you have useful information to pass on to customers who need your expert opinion.

Cultural Evaluation

This is concerned with the quality of the writing and the style. It may be difficult to be completely objective about this as we all have preferences, but essentially you should be trying to assess if it is suitable to the subject matter.

The Market

However interesting, worthy or valuable a title may be, you have to decide whether or not you can sell it to your customers. You are the link between the author and the reader, but not all books can be sold in all shops; you have to be selective according to your known market.

Customers can be broadly classified as book buyers into a number of categories, none mutually exclusive. These are general and recreational readers, children, people with hobbies, students of all ages, vocational readers (those who want books in connection with their work), writers both amateur and professional, research specialists, and scholars.

Try to determine into which broad categories your customers may fall. Other categories may be appropriate to specialist shops; for example a religious bookseller would probably see a natural division between clergy and laity.

You will also need to consider why people buy books and why they don't. There is a wide range of answers to such questions but you need to focus on those that are particular to your community or catchment area.

Books can also be said to fall into a number of broad-brush categories, for example reference, standard work, primer or introduction, popular works, gift books, textbooks, children's books and monographs. What may be a gift book to one customer may be a reference book to another or collectable as a series to another; none of these headings is mutually exclusive. Some children's books have a place in the adult sections and vice versa.

In many cases the decision to take a book may depend not only on evaluation but on receiving satisfactory terms from the publisher. In other instances, the question may be whether the book is suitable for the stock image the bookshop wishes to project, although this should be market-based and not founded on personal preference or prejudice. What other books are in competition with it? When will it be published? How long will it take to sell? What media coverage and advertising is expected? Such matters have to be considered along with the specific evaluation points made above.

Special Arrangements

If additional copies are required for a special reason such as the window promotion of a title or a signing session, these can be ordered 'see safe'. This signifies that the bookseller is invoiced for the books on delivery, but permission to send back unsold copies after an agreed time, usually three months, will be granted and a credit note issued in due course.* In cash flow terms, the bookseller would be best advised to insist on buying only the quantity actually required, and to limit the use of 'see safe' – it is often called the lazy buyer's get-out clause. Some publishers may require a replacement order to the same value as the books being returned, rather than being prepared to issue a credit note. This may well result in further unsuitable stock being represented, especially in a specialist bookshop or department.

Books are rarely ordered 'on sale or return' as these are dealt with in the same way as 'see safe'. Historically 'on sale' meant the publisher would supply the books on a delivery note, and would only invoice the copies actually sold after the agreed period and after any returns had been made. This was more easily possible when invoicing was handled manually by the publisher, but does not fit into computerised systems.

These terms are used rather loosely and interchangeably in the trade and it is advisable to be quite clear with each publisher what is meant when ordering on this basis. A bookseller may also request a publisher to supply a copy of a book 'on approval' to show a customer; the copy will be invoiced and credited if returned. In all cases, delivery or carriage charges will be invoiced by the publisher to the bookseller if appropriate to the size of

*Sometimes reps will try to push buyers into taking extra copies on this basis.

order, and usually the bookseller will bear the cost of carriage on any books returned for credit.

Order Forms

If the bookseller decides to use his own order form rather than the BA Standard Order Form (Fig. 2), then the design should include the following information:–

a) the bookshop's name and address (usually printed)
b) the publisher's name
c) Standard Address Number (SAN) – a unique reference for each bookshop
d) bookseller's order number/reference – usually printed on top right hand corner, but sometimes in a left hand margin where individual references appear against each item
e) date (of despatch) or order
f) quantity
g) author and title
h) price/edition
i) ISBN (see p.115)
j) any special instructions – if the book is to be sent to a customer direct, include an addressed label
k) invoice address if different from ordering address
l) other instructions such as whether the order should be cancelled or recorded if unavailable

The order form should be typed if possible or at least written neatly. It should include space for the publisher to add any necessary editing to facilitate picking of stock from the warehouse and the invoicing procedures used.

Orders can be sent to publishers in a variety of ways. Direct to the rep has already been mentioned; for urgent orders, first-class post direct to the publisher can be used, or telephone, fax or telex. However, not all publishers handle their own distribution, in which case the order should be sent to the distributor; it is advisable to maintain up-to-date and accurate records of publishers and their distribution. There are two invaluable publications, namely, The Booksellers Association's *Directory of British Publishers and Wholesalers* and Whitaker's *Publishers in the United Kingdom and their Addresses*.

ORDER

PLEASE RETURN YELLOW COPY ORDER WITH BOOKS AND/OR REPORTS

TO

FROM

STANDARD ADDRESS No.

Always QUOTE ORDER No.

757406

DATE POSTED

CONSIGNMENT ADDRESS (IF DIFFERENT)

SPECIAL INSTRUCTIONS

CUSTOMER'S REF.	QUANTITY	ISBN	TITLE, SERIES, AUTHOR	H/Bk P/Bk OR PRICE	PUBLISHER'S USE

Fig. 2 The BA Standard Order Form.

An alternative cheaper method is to route orders through a clearing house, such as BOD (Booksellers Orders Distribution) or IBIS Orders Clearing. To use such a service, booksellers send all their orders in one envelope to the clearing house which sorts and redirects them to the appropriate publisher by first-class post. A monthly invoice is sent from the clearing house showing the total number of orders distributed, this being well below the cost of second-class postage on individual orders if sent direct to the publisher.

Some booksellers will order all their requirements from wholesalers; others will mix their ordering, placing some orders with the publisher and some with a wholesaler according to the business, particularly being conscious of delivery times. The discount from wholesalers may not be as good as that obtainable from the publisher, but speed of service is likely to offset that consideration.

Teleordering

Teleordering is an electronic ordering facility, and in the UK (administered by Teleordering Ltd) is based on the use of an 'intelligent' terminal (or PC) based in the bookshop (see Fig. 3 on pages 26–7). Orders are keyed into this (by ISBN or author/title and publisher) and then transmitted overnight by telephone line to a central computer, which transmits the order direct to the publisher's computer if that publisher is electronically linked, or otherwise sends it in printed form to the publisher. The Teleordering system can also be used by larger booksellers who have their own mini or mainframe computer. In these cases, the bookseller controls the transmission of his orders. For the smaller bookseller a Viewdata system is also available.

The advantages of the system for the bookseller include:

a) Reduction in delivery times providing customers with improved service
b) Reduction in delivery times leading to more efficient stock turn
c) Reduction in in-shop paperwork
d) Minimising publishers' small-order surcharges
e) More efficient use of staff time within the bookshop.

In simple terms, the procedures in the bookshop are as follows:

a) Orders are entered by ISBN, or author, title and publisher/distributor with the SAN, at times convenient to the bookseller throughout the day
b) Orders are checked and stored by the bookseller's terminal
c) The terminal memory is emptied overnight by the central computer which telephones each terminal; this is all automatic and is termed 'polling'
d) Confirmation of the order, and reports of any books not available, are produced centrally and passed back to the terminal for printing out the next morning
e) There is a 'bulking' facility which enables the bookseller to hold individual orders for one publisher until the aggregate is sufficient to minimise small-order surcharges.

The central computer processes the information received against Whitaker's *Books in Print*, checks SANs and ISBNs and expands the latter into full bibliographic information if necessary, sorts all orders in publisher sequence, adds bookshop details and passes that information back to the bookseller. This system provides cost-effective savings for the bookseller, who should not react against what may seem to be high initial costs.

Small Orders

Customers often expect booksellers to stock every title they may require, not realising that there are 560 000 books in print. Taking special orders for a single copy is an essential part of the bookseller's service, but that does produce its own problems, as many small orders are subject to penalty surcharges if below a certain value. Either a small-order surcharge is imposed, or a reduced discount is given or packing and postage is levied. Economically, both publisher and bookseller have a problem with this type of order, and yet such orders are the lifeblood of good service to the customer. Because of resale price maintenance (where the price is usually printed on the book), many booksellers feel unable to pass the surcharge on to the customer, although some do so. With any other commodity such surcharges would be built into the price quoted. So goodwill often prevails over commercial judgement. In some instances the 'special' order may be a stock replacement, so the single can be increased to avoid the surcharge.

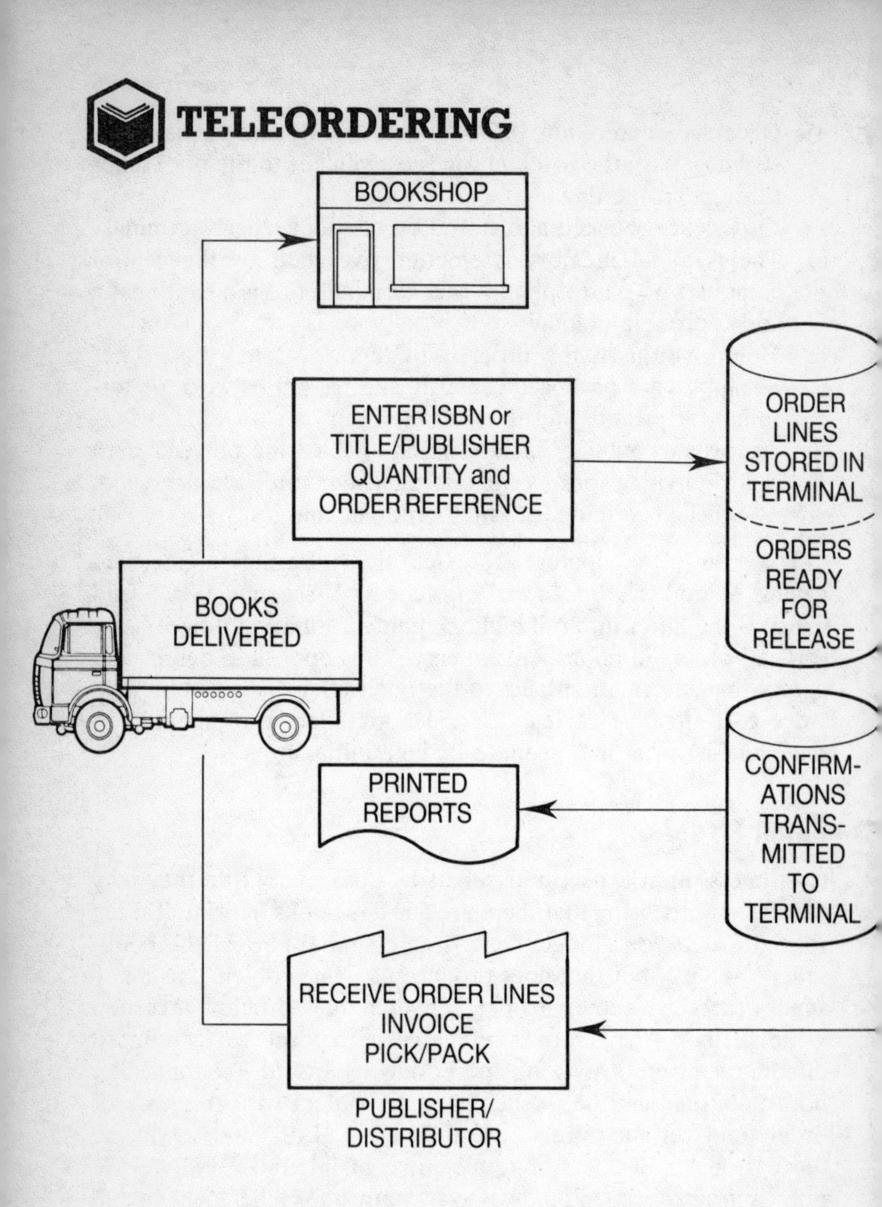

Fig. 3 The UK Teleordering system.

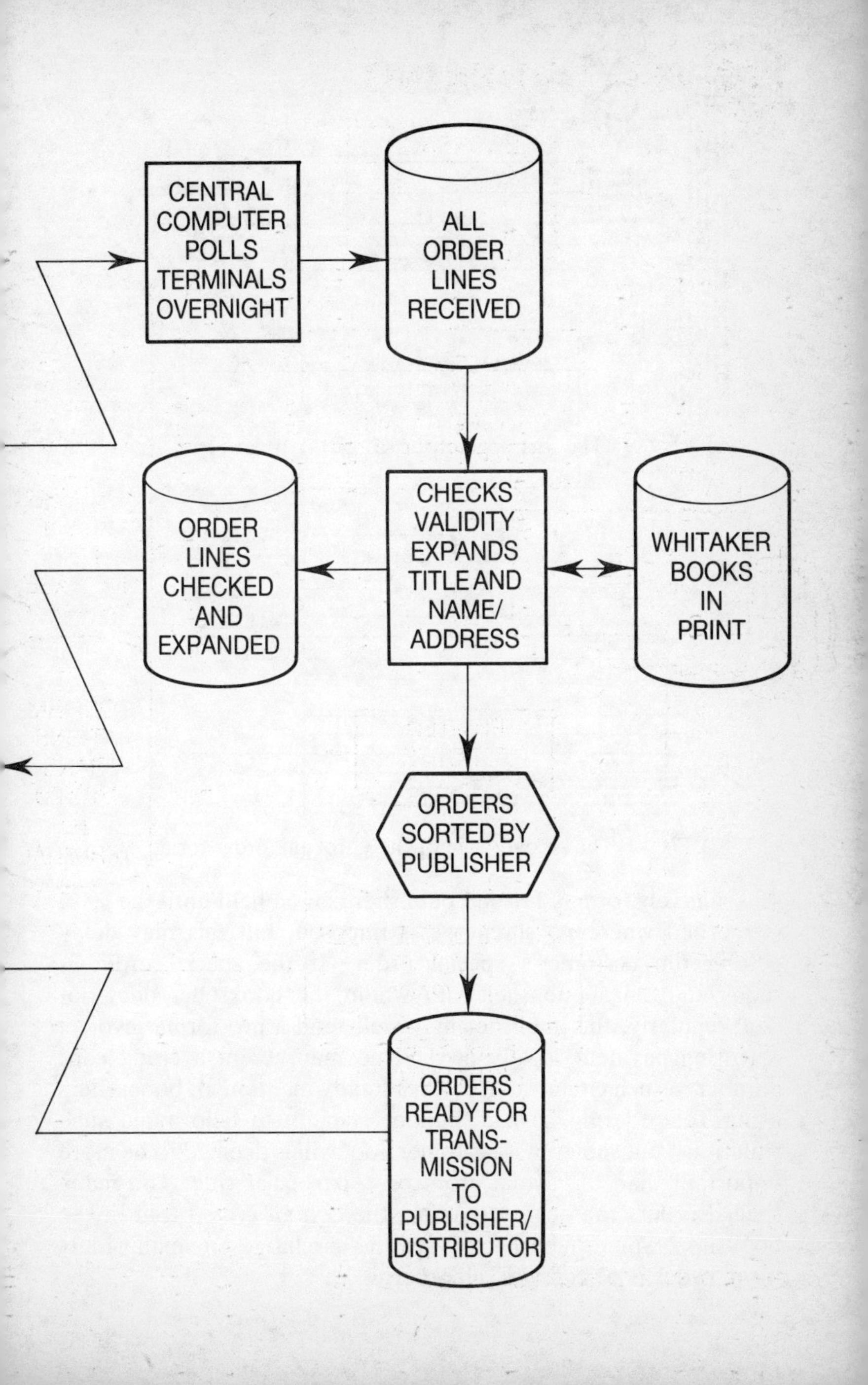

CENTRAL COMPUTER POLLS TERMINALS OVERNIGHT
ALL ORDER LINES RECEIVED
ORDER LINES CHECKED AND EXPANDED
CHECKS VALIDITY EXPANDS TITLE AND NAME/ ADDRESS
WHITAKER BOOKS IN PRINT
ORDERS SORTED BY PUBLISHER
ORDERS READY FOR TRANS- MISSION TO PUBLISHER/ DISTRIBUTOR

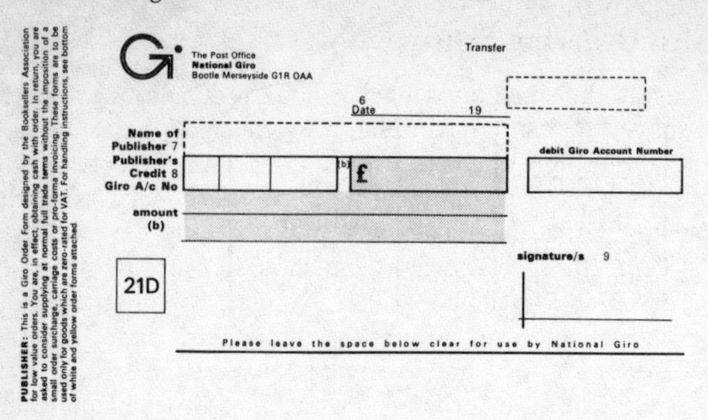

PUBLISHER: This is a Giro Order Form designed by the Booksellers Association for low value orders. You are, in effect, obtaining cash with order. In return, you are asked to consider supplying at normal full trade terms without the imposition of a small order surcharge, carriage costs or pro-forma invoicing. These forms are to be used only for goods which are zero-rated for VAT. For handling instructions, see bottom of white and yellow order forms attached.

The Post Office
National Giro
Bootle Merseyside G1R 0AA

Transfer

6 Date 19

Name of Publisher 7
Publisher's Credit 8 **Giro A/c No**

(b) £

debit Giro Account Number

amount (b)

signature/s 9

21D

Please leave the space below clear for use by National Giro

Fig. 4a The first page of the Girobank order form.

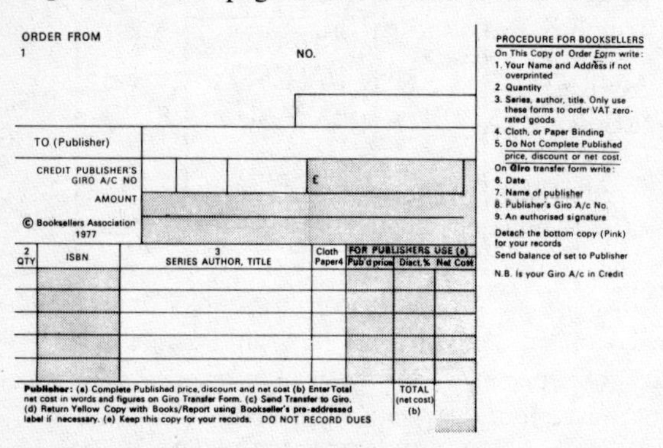

ORDER FROM
1

NO.

TO (Publisher)

CREDIT PUBLISHER'S GIRO A/C NO £

AMOUNT

© Booksellers Association 1977

2 QTY	ISBN	3 SERIES AUTHOR, TITLE	Cloth Paper4	FOR PUBLISHERS USE (a) Pub'd price	Disct.%	Net Cost

Publisher: (a) Complete Published price, discount and net cost (b) Enter Total net cost in words and figures on Giro Transfer Form. (c) Send Transfer to Giro. (d) Return Yellow Copy with Books/Report using Bookseller's pre-addressed label if necessary. (e) Keep this copy for your records. DO NOT RECORD DUES

TOTAL (net cost) (b)

PROCEDURE FOR BOOKSELLERS
On This Copy of Order Form write:
1. Your Name and Address if not overprinted
2. Quantity
3. Series, author, title. Only use these forms to order VAT zero-rated goods
4. Cloth, or Paper Binding
5. Do Not Complete Published price, discount or net cost.

On Giro transfer form write:
6. Date
7. Name of publisher
8. Publisher's Giro A/c No.
9. An authorised signature

Detach the bottom copy (Pink) for your records
Send balance of set to Publisher

N.B. Is your Giro A/c in Credit

Fig. 4b The second page of the Girobank order form.

Alternatively, orders for one publisher can be held until the level is reached where no surcharge is imposed, but this may delay getting the customer's special order. If the special order is required from a publisher with whom the bookseller does not deal regularly, the publisher may well send a pro forma invoice, requiring payment in advance. Some may accept a credit card number in such circumstances. As already mentioned, booksellers using Teleordering have a 'bulking' facility to help avoid such situations, but sometimes customer goodwill is deemed to be more important than the actual profit on a particular title. Too many special orders can adversely affect the overall gross profit of the bookshop. Some publishers waive the surcharge on small orders if the order is placed via Teleordering.

BA Giro Ordering Scheme

Of interest to the small bookseller, who in particular may find his orders subject to surcharges because of the small order value, is the Giro Ordering System (see Figs 4a and 4b for examples of order forms). This was designed by the Booksellers Association and the Post Office National Giro, and is in effect a cash-with-order system; the special order form should ensure that the best terms are available to the bookseller for small, usually single copy orders. The scheme can, however, only be used if the publisher and bookseller run accounts with the National Giro Bank. It is also possible to use an ordinary Post Office Giro cheque but if you select this method you lose the benefit of having a record of the order, which is provided by the BA multi-form system.

Ordering From Overseas

For the bookseller who regularly orders from overseas direct from publishers, it will be necessary to devise lightweight orders for air mail use. The bookseller who seldom places such orders will probably prefer to use an agent in this country or a wholesaler in the overseas country concerned. It should be remembered that the delivery may be slow, although wholesalers in particular in countries like Germany often deliver faster than many UK publishers. Procedures for handling the order on arrival will be similar except that the price will need to be calculated, not only at the current conversion rate for that currency but also to include the bank charges that are involved which can often cancel any profit, especially if only one invoice is to be paid. Bank charges should be spread over a number of invoices if possible, as only one bank draft need then be drawn.

Distribution

One of the problems that has always concerned the trade is the time it takes from the date the bookseller places the order to the date of receipt. This causes problems with customers who fail to understand why it can take at least 3–4 weeks (though many provide a better service) to obtain a particular book; the record industry can deliver in 24–48 hours, so why the problem in the book trade? If there was an easy answer, there would be no need to comment. We have already looked at the various ways in which an order can be placed and how the order can be routed to the publisher. There is an immediate in-built delay, although some systems are better than others. A special order placed by a customer which requires bibliographical research may not be turned into an order to the publisher until the following day, and even using the fastest methods is unlikely to reach the publisher until the third day. Most booksellers trade six days a week, whereas publishers' warehouses operate on a five day basis, Monday to Friday. Despite what we have said about well-designed or standard order forms, there are still booksellers who do not use such forms, and these cause the publisher problems which may well delay other orders in the pipeline.

The typical publisher's 'post room' will receive large numbers of orders daily which will need sorting before 'editing', a process of selecting, revising and arranging the information on the order prior to entry to the computer. Use of Teleordering and ISBNs facilitates this process but not all orders received include that information. Many orders will be badly written and not typed as suggested earlier. It will also be necessary to check the credit-worthiness or the state of account of the bookseller at this stage.

The computer will produce the invoice and an order-picking note which is used to match the stock in the warehouse to the bookseller's order. Computers can produce the invoice to match the actual picking order in the warehouse. Bulk stocks have to be physically brought forward; warehousing in many cases is a sophisticated and automated procedure, but this varies from publisher to publisher. Booksellers perhaps fail to appreciate the problems for publishers at the picking stage with hundreds (sometimes thousands) of different titles having to be brought together and married up to the bookseller's order and the publisher's invoice for that order. Once collated and checked, the order will need to be packed and then the carrier route planned. Each bookseller only sees his order in terms of his own customers, and does not always appreciate that the order he is worried about is going through the warehouse process with hundreds of other orders from both home and overseas, apart from the new publications also being processed. Much of the delay in the books reaching the bookseller occurs at the carrier stage. This is often seen as a book trade problem but is in fact a national problem; streamlining of handling and improvements of routing do not always produce a speedier service, although they may prove to be cost-effective to the carrier on a national or local scale.

Unavailable Titles

It is inevitable that at times the publisher is unable to supply the book required by the bookseller, because it is not available. When this happens the publisher sends a 'report' or 'answer', which will either be given on the invoice or separately. Many publishers use numerical codes to represent the actual words. The most frequently used answers are as follows:

a) **RP/** reprinting; this means that the publisher has to arrange for the pages to be printed and the books to be bound. RP/ is usually qualified by additions explaining this more fully, e.g.
   RP/ND means reprinting, no date for re-issue.
   RP/June indicates that the book will be ready again in June – an alternative to this is RP/6 indicating June, the sixth month of the year.
   RP/2m meaning that the book will be available in two months.
   RP/UC stands for reprint under consideration; publishers will follow this answer with a definite one when a decision has been taken.
b) **Bdg or B/** means binding; that implies that the publisher has spare sets of pages in stock but has to have these bound, i.e. have the covers fitted. This answer will also be qualified in the same way as RP/ described above.
c) **NYP** or **NP** standing for Not yet published or Not published; again such an answer will be qualified with an indication of when the title will be available.
d) **NE** means new edition; may or may not be qualified as already described.
e) **OO/** out of stock but on order from abroad, e.g. OO/USA.
f) **OTO/** only to order with the country specified e.g. OTO/France. Having been informed of the possible delay in delivery, the bookseller must usually confirm that he wants the order placed.

g) **OP** means out of print; technically this means it will never be issued again, but the answer is used rather loosely by some publishers who should more accurately use O/P/P, out of print for the present, or a variation T/O/P, temporarily out of print.
h) **NK** means not known. This in itself can mean a number of things; it may be a very old book from that publisher of which no records exist; it may be a forthcoming title that is not yet listed or it may mean it is not known because someone else publishes it. Sometimes NOP – not our publication – is used.

The recommended numerical codes for these answers are as follows:

1 Not known
2 On order to follow (qualified by a date)
3 Binding
4 Reprinting
5 Not yet published
6 New edition in preparation
7 Reprint under consideration
8 Out of print
9 On order abroad

It must be emphasised that for many customers, especially librarians, accurate reports are essential; it is not satisfactory to leave checking this until someone has a spare moment. Knowing that a title is not obtainable is as important to some customers as having the book supplied, as they can at least try other sources. Copies may not be available from the publisher but could be via a wholesaler, and certainly at some other bookshop although they may take a long time to track down.

Stock Ordering

The investment in stock and its consequences is dealt with in the financial section of this book. The range of stock displayed will be at the discretion of the buyer, but should reflect the needs of the local market, and any speciality the bookshop wishes to promote. Whatever decisions are taken, they must reflect real need rather than the personal preferences (even prejudices) of the buyer, who inevitably wants to stamp something of himself on the image of the shop. Regular stock checking will ensure that the publishers' back lists are represented, but with the high output of titles it may be necessary to vary the stock, particularly of well-known and popular authors. For example, if an author has written twenty titles in paperback, it is usually unrealistic to stock all at any one time. Six separate titles may be selected, sold out and replaced with six others, although some titles will always need to be displayed. A varying stock is of interest to the regular customer who does not want to see the same titles over and over again. Changes in market demand can be assessed through special orders and by talking to customers; also useful is a 'stock refused' list on which is noted every title to which the bookshop says 'No' to a customer. It does not follow that the buyer has to order that title immediately but such a list may give hints of changing trends in demand, which can be useful in the future.

It might sound simple to say that regular checking of stock and careful monitoring of refused titles will help to give a balanced stock. This would be far too easy an answer and far too general an approach. To eliminate guessing how many copies to buy, and how frequently those copies need to be replaced, we need to be much more sophisticated in our methods. In short, we need some form of control. This is covered in the following chapter.

3

Stock Control

Stock control is the bookseller's method of making sure he has the right books in the right quantity at the right time. Too few or too many can mean poor sales on the one hand, or too much money tied up in stock on the other. If these extremes become obvious to the customer, because there simply isn't enough of a range on show, or because too many books make the place overcrowded, sales can be lost. If titles are not replaced when they should be, the eventual outcome is that only those books which don't sell remain, and stock which could sell again and again is not repeated.

Before the individual titles and sections can be controlled, an initial value for the total stock must be set. This overall figure should bear a relationship to the value of sales expected in the current year. Without this overall figure to start with, there will be no recognisable limit to the amount of buying the bookseller can afford, and his daily stock control may lead him into over-investment and difficulties.

The total investment in stock can be measured and controlled in two ways:

a) by the value of the stock as a retail or cost total, and
b) by the quantity and range of titles in the shop from day to day.

A bookshop is said to 'turn over' its stock each year, the assumption being that if your books sell on average four copies a year, then your stock turn for that title is four annually, usually expressed as 4:1. Above that figure in a small general bookshop is considered to be good, though in terms of profit and growth 4:1 is a low target. Naturally, not every book is successful and some may not sell at all. To achieve an average stock turn of 4, many books must sell a great deal more than 4 copies to help the overall picture. The art and aim is to increase this higher number whilst keeping down the number of slower sellers which keep the stock turn down.

The need to turn over stock at this rate is a matter of investment. If you buy £25 000-worth of books (at retail) to start a bookshop, you should expect to sell £100 000 in value in a year. To achieve these sales you will have spent the cost element of £25 000 (about £16 000) on stock; as you sell, so your money returns and you can buy more stock. If you buy successfully, you need not spend more than the original £16 000, so your investment is under control. If you buy badly, or buy too many books, your investment begins to grow larger than your ability to pay, or borrow. It is quite possible to buy £20 000-worth of stock (£30 000 at retail) and still only achieve the annual £100 000 in turnover. You will have spent £4000 more on stock than you need have done, and your stock-turn ratio will have fallen to just above three.

Using our model bookshop, let's say that you expect to sell £250 000-worth of books in a year. A stock turn of four means that you expect to have about a quarter of your annual sales in stock at any one time – in this case, about £62 500 at retail prices. If you start with this amount, then measuring is quite simple.

If we sell £5000 in the first week, you are left with £57 500. To keep track of the fluctuations in this figure – some weeks will be higher, some much lower – total each week's purchase invoices by their *retail* value. Add this figure to the £57 500 to get a new total, subtract the following week's sales, then add the week's purchases, and so on. This process is repeated each week and you can therefore keep a weekly track of your total retail investment.

Example:

	£	
Starting retail stock figure	62 500	
First week's sales	5 000	SUBTRACT
subtotal	57 500	
First week's purchases	1 500	ADD
New stock figure	59 000	
Second week's sales	4 300	SUBTRACT
subtotal	54 700	
Second week's purchases	6 000	ADD
New stock figure	60 700	

NB: All figures are retail; it would be fatal to confuse retail and cost prices!

The knack is not to re-order more books than you will need for future sales, and to keep your investment total clearly in mind.

What about Christmas and other seasonal peaks of the year? You will need more books for these busy times, and assessing and budgeting seasonal orders is dealt with later in this chapter. But again, you must not buy more than the season demands: if you expect to take £50 000 during December, it is pointless ordering more than that in value beforehand – you are bound to be left with unwanted stock. In fact it is much wiser to *under*-order because many books already in stock will sell at Christmas, and there is no need to buy in completely fresh stock.

It is usually the shop manager's job to keep track of the total value of stock; the ordering and re-ordering of individual titles may well be the responsibility of shop staff, who have closer contact with daily sales and customer needs. Not keeping track of the sale of books by title must eventually lead to bad stock, too much stock, and worse, no stock of the books which might have sold if they had been on the shelves.

A shop with £62 500 on the shelves will have about 9000 titles in stock; it is impossible for one person to keep track of such a range other than by using a stock control method. About 80% of the range will be basic items which will need re-ordering; about 20% will be new titles, which may or may not be successful enough to become regularly stocked. Some of the stock items may have been badly chosen in the first place, and need to be forgotten once sold, though they could have been bought with very short-term sales in mind. Some may be regular sellers, and need to be replaced; some may sell, but so slowly that it is better to put the same money into a book which is more popular. Controlling these permutations has to be mechanised to get the maximum benefit for the bookseller and the customer.

What methods are there? The most obvious answer is a small computer, and there are stock control programs which have been specifically designed for booksellers. Let's return to that subject after considering the alternatives.

Stock Cards

A file card is made out for every title: the entries are systematic, showing author, title, publisher, edition, price and subject. The cards may be kept in alphabetical order (by author) for the whole stock, or broken down into shop subjects and then put in alphabetical order by author. The latter method can lead to confusion because staff will have different ideas about which books are carried in what sections.

STOCK CONTROL CARD – DO NOT REMOVE

AUTHOR: ELLIOTT, GREY + MILLER | PUBLISHER: HODDER + STOUGHTON

TITLE: TEACH YOURSELF BOOKSELLING | ISBN 0 3 4 0 4 2 8 7 6 7

PUB. CATEGORY | REORDER LEVEL 2 | MAX. STOCK: 5 | PRICE: £3.99

TV | FILM | RADIO | OU | GCSE | REC. TEXT | SECTION: TEACH YOURSELF / CAREERS + BUSINESS

DATE	STOCK	Quantity ordered	DATE ordered (or O/No)	DATE received (or Report)	SALES	DATE	STOCK	Quantity ordered	DATE ordered (or O/No)	DATE received (or Report)	SALES
SuB	3/9/89		6 ✓	4/3/90							
5/4/90	2	3	6/4/90	28/4/90	4						

Fig. 5 A typical stock control card.

Sales of books are recorded as the customer pays for them and the date of sale entered on the card when the day's sales are accounted for. If stock falls to zero or a low point, sales in a given period can be calculated, which in turn suggests how many need to be re-ordered, if any. The number ordered is entered along with the date and when the books arrive, that date is also entered on the stock card. If the books don't arrive, the reason can be entered on the card. Books are not always available all the time: they may be being reprinted or a new edition may be in preparation. Finally, of course, the title may go out of print altogether.

The problem with this manual system, though it has been a basic method in bookselling for many years, is the time it takes. There is also the problems of how to record the sales which are made. If you don't record daily sales, then all the cards must be regularly checked against the shop stock, simply to find out what has sold. This means that many books are checked many times over to no avail.

You can write down the titles as they are sold on a pad kept at the counter for the purpose. But at busy times this can get overlooked, or can take too long for queueing customers. You can keep another card in the back of the book, to be removed when the book is sold. But this takes time, because then two cards must be made out for each book. Also, they may fall out when browsers look at the book.

Tape Recorder

One good method is to tape-record details of the books as they are sold – recording author, title and publisher for playback later in the day or first thing in the morning. The advantage of a tape recorder is that you can keep a note of titles you have had to refuse, or those which have been suggested by other staff, or discovered because a customer has ordered it specially. The tape recorder can also be used as a jotter or diary.

The playback is self-editing, in that titles which you may have recorded several times in a day need only be written down once: you only need one reminder that the book has sold. The resulting list can be taken to the shelves and marked according to what stock, if any, is left. If there are plenty, the title can be crossed off. The final short-list is of those you need to check against the stock card.

The system has the advantage that you are checking your *moving* stock *daily*, so you can replace titles quickly. The list can (and should) be checked by any member of staff, and helps to familiarise new staff with the range which the shop carries.

Computer Stock Control

These manual systems will do the job required of them, but are repetitive and subject to individual error and loss. There are better things to do with valuable staff and management time. Any new bookshop should invest in a small computer as a matter of course, and as part of the initial investment. Not only can the machine be used for stock control but for accounts too, and perhaps invoicing and letter-writing in due course. Learning to use the system may take time, but it is well spent: a great deal more time will be spent over the months and years in daily stock checking.

Stock control programs can do much more than simply record the sale of a book: some make calculations about future sales and the stock needed to make those sales. The machine can be linked to Teleordering (see p. 24), so that orders entered can be automatically transmitted and recorded. The program may be linked to a bibliographic database: selecting and ordering a title for a customer or for stock can be done in the same operation. It can really be said that a computer is essential, unless your shop is very small.

Ordering For Seasonal Peaks

Ordering as you go along is a relatively easy habit to adopt, once your system is bedded in. But for Christmas, orders need to be placed well in advance, usually as early as September. Academic booksellers needing to stock their textbooks for the October term should place their orders in June and July. And booksellers who also sell greetings cards will place their Christmas card orders by the Easter beforehand.

Christmas can be an awkward period to buy for: most general and gift publishing is directed towards this time of the year and the late summer and early autumn sees the production of many books clearly designed to sell in December, and perhaps at no other time. These books will be bought gradually from reps, and in larger quantities than would be involved at any other time of year. Everyday stock lines also increase their sales dramatically at the end of the year: cookery, gardening, do-it-yourself, travel, health care, reference, history titles and new hardback fiction all sell in quantity, and orders for these will be drawn from stock records in September. Sales for Christmas can begin in October – many people plan to buy their gifts early for Christmas, and books destined for relatives overseas must be sent very early if they are to arrive in time.

The need to budget for Christmas purchases is vital: to buy too much for this relatively short period is to invite disaster. Unsold Christmas titles are notoriously difficult to shift in January and February. Returning them to the publisher – possible, and often offered as an inducement to purchase in the run-up to December – is expensive, and your cash is still tied up with your supplier in the form of credit notes, until they eventually arrive. The very high bills with which you may be faced at the end of January may not be met by cash in the bank – Christmas is not always a boom time for everyone.

So there is even more need to have an annual budget broken down into months. In this way you can tell that November and December require just so much purchasing, and no more. Our model budget on page 66 shows that we can expect £90 000 in cash sales in the two months. Some of this will be ordinary daily sales, some will be special orders not related to the gift market. The average month's cash takings of £9000 at any other time of the year shows that about £18 000 in November and December sales will be everyday stock lines, usually in stock and accounted for by daily stock control.

It's important to note here that the invoice sales in these two months – and any other month in the year – cannot be purchase-budgeted in the same way. These sales are presumed to be orders which school or commercial customers place with the bookshop. They must be *anticipated* in the budget, but you don't place orders for these books until the customer actually orders them, so they do not form part of your advance ordering plans.

This leaves £72 000 in retail sales which might be attributable to Christmas itself, and caution suggests that, in terms of advance buying commitments, this figure could be reduced to £60 000. For the remaining potential £12 000, wholesalers will come into their own, with very fast service on just those new titles which you felt were borderline decisions when first shown by the rep in September and October. The one tantalising feature about the big titles for this time of the year is that no-one really knows which title is going to be number one, and there are often surprises in this bestselling range. A particularly good review on TV or radio, or an unexpected newspaper serialisation, even the return of an old programme favourite can push a book to the front of stage at just the right time.

The £60 000 retail figure we have reached will be £40 000 or thereabouts at cost. The normal 80/20 ratio of back stock to new titles alters at Christmas to something more like 50/50; so the stock order in September is going to cost about £20 000 in our model business, and may be spread over a dozen suppliers in the main. They will normally be ready to negotiate longer periods of payment, so that stock can be ordered in time to ensure sales, but payment need not be made until probably the end of January.

An established bookshop with good stock control will of course have last year's records to show what sold and what did not. The progress of the shop during the current year will indicate whether or not these figures should be increased. For example, if the shop has shown a regular 10% growth in sales between January and August, then it would be reasonable to suppose that last year's Christmas ordering, for the right titles, can be increased by 10%.

Staff should be involved as much as possible with ordering decisions, and be aware of the incoming stock range. Sales are lost at this time of the year because customers buying gifts want to make sure of their purchases and will shop around more than usual, often not being prepared to wait for stock to come in again.

The remaining £20 000 will be spent in budgeted purchase sessions with reps as they call. There will be everyday titles to consider as well as gift books, but apart from the fact that ordering will be spread over a longer period than the September stock order, the same principles apply. So you will be spending about £2000 each with the ten companies you might choose to supply you with their principal titles, and the decisions beyond this budgeting exercise fall to the criteria discussed in Chapter 1 on buying new books.

Bargain Books

There will be some ranges which do not need specific title control; bargain books (also known as remainders) are those sold by the publisher as reduced price items from his back list. If a publisher produces 10 000 copies of a book and finds from his own stock control that the last 1000 copies will take a year or more to sell, then it is in his interests to sell the book much more cheaply to get rid of the stock, bring in as much cash as he can as quickly as possible, and make way for new titles. The 1000-odd copies will be made available either through his own reps or more likely through a remainder dealer, or jobber, who will buy all 1000 at once. Margins on these books used to be higher than is now generally the case, but 35–40% should be entirely possible for a small bookshop which orders reasonable quantities. Such books, even though priced at about half their original retail price, sell only with market-style display methods, with stacked piles and reduction tickets much in evidence. Such books are not faulty in any way and should be in good condition – many will sell as Christmas gifts.

Some publishing is based on the likelihood that a book will 'remainder' at the end of its life. So a publisher will print, say, 15 000 in the knowledge that he will have made a good profit after selling 12 000 copies. He is then free either to remainder the title or to carry on with a slower rate of sale at the normal full price. This kind of publishing relies on the fact that the more copies of a title are printed at one go, the lower the individual copy cost.

The purchase of bargain books still needs cost budgeting, even if it forms only an occasional part of the buying and selling decisions in the shop.

Perhaps the simplest illustration of the need for stock control is the fact that in a small, restricted-budget company, the purchase of three copies of a book, of which only two actually sell, means that that buying decision has made no profit at all. Look:

3 copies @ £5.95 each	£17.85
the cost is	£11.90
2 copies sold @ £5.95	£11.90

The remaining copy holds all the profit.

4

Bookshop Accounting

By law, the running of a business – usually a limited company in bookselling – must be annually assessed by independent accountants who can vouch that the company is being run on a proper financial footing. The firm's accountant will advise on any aspect of financial control during the year, and is responsible for auditing the annual accounts. But the work of providing the basis for these figures is done by the owner in a shop the size of our example; larger shops may employ a full-time financial assistant or director.

Management Accounts

Very simply, the method of accounting for the income and outgoings of the company is twofold: 1) the budget created by the shop owner, which lays out plans for expected income and expenses, and cash-flow; and 2) the actual results as the company progresses through the year.

Keeping in daily contact with the finances of the business means regular reports are necessary, and many companies now create monthly statements of income and expenditure called management accounts.

These management accounts often incorporate the original budget, which has itself been created on a monthly basis, shown at the side of the actual results for comparison. It is then clear if there are worrying or encouraging departures from any income or expense figure. An example set of management accounts is shown on p. 45.

These figures can be drawn up for each quarter but, with the advent of cheap packages for personal computers, there is little harm in keeping accounts even more up-to-date. It is unwise to leave such reviews for any longer than three months because problem trends are more difficult to reverse if not discovered straight away; to wait for annual results is to court disaster.

Margins

The terms 'gross margin' and 'gross profit' are frequently used in retailing and need explanation. The gross margin on a sale is the difference between the cost of buying the book from its supplier (publisher or wholesaler), and its retail price to the customer. Thus a book selling at a retail price of £12.95 may be bought at a cost price of £8.42; the difference in value is £4.53, a gross margin of 35%.

Gross profit as a term is not normally used to represent the profit on the sale of a single book, but on the sale of all books in a given period – a week, month or year. Whilst many books may sell at the full 35% margin, many more may sell at lesser levels of margin. Some may be ordered for customers in single copies and therefore attract postage or handling charges. Some may be technical books which earn low discounts on the retail price. The effect of selling books with mixed margins is to reduce the overall gross profit on the sales.

The following shows the result of selling books with mixed margins:

	Retail price	*Cost price*	*Handling charge*	*Margin*
	£	£	£	
	12.95	8.42	0	35%
	25.00	18.75	1.00	21%
	5.00	3.50	0	30%
	4.95	3.31	0	33%
Totals	47.90	33.98	1.00	27%

In this example, the gross margins are variable and produce a gross *profit* which is quite different again from the invoiced margins allowed by the supplier. If normal stock orders are placed anticipating a minimum 33%, these figures show that the true mix

Management Accounts Model

Month: May

	£ Budget	£ Actual	£ Variance
Cash	44000	42000	−2000
Invoices	25500	28000	2500
TOTAL	69500	70000	500
GROSS PROFIT	20015	20020	5
	28.80%	28.60%	−0.20%
Rent	5000	5000	0
Rates	1665	1665	0
Salaries	12914	12550	364
Post	460	500	−40
Print	750	500	250
Phone	415	300	115
Fuel	250	315	−65
Motor	166	262	−96
Audit	730	0	730
Bank charges	1190	650	540
Depreciation	1250	1250	0
Repairs	250	62	188
Cleaning	500	513	−13
Computer	625	400	225
Subscriptions	315	440	−125
Advertising	835	329	506
Petty cash	415	390	25
TOTALS	27730	25126	2604
NET PROFIT	−7715	−5106	2584

Notes

This model shows the set of figures which a shop manager or accountant might produce for the bookshop trading up to May of the year we have exampled elsewhere.

The Budget column shows all expected figures for sales and expenses up to and including the month of May. The Actual column shows what actually happened, with the variances shown in the right-hand column.

It can be seen that the business expected to have made a loss of £7715, but that matters had improved by £2584, and the eventual shortfall was only £5106. Losses can be acceptable if they are anticipated, and if the figures remain on target, profitable months can be expected to arrive on time. If the figures show greater losses than planned, then action to create sales or cut expenses may be necessary.

Margin variance models

Model A

£000	*Total*	*Jan*	*Feb*	*Mar*	*Apr*	*May*	*June*	*July*	*Aug*	*Sept*	*Oct*	*Nov*	*Dec*
Cash (35%)	200	12.0	7.0	7.0	10.0	8.0	10.0	8.0	8.0	10.0	30.0	40.0	50.0
Invoices (25%)	50	2.3	6.6	1.5	7.5	7.5	1.0	0.5	7.6	6.5	1.0	5.5	2.5
ALL SALES	250	14.3	13.6	8.5	17.5	15.4	11.0	8.5	15.6	16.5	31.0	45.5	52.5
Gross profit	82.5	4.8	4.1	2.8	5.4	4.7	3.8	2.9	4.7	5.1	10.8	15.4	18.1
Percentage	33.0%												

Model B

£000	*Total*	*Jan*	*Feb*	*Mar*	*Apr*	*May*	*June*	*July*	*Aug*	*Sept*	*Oct*	*Nov*	*Dec*
Cash (33%)	200	12.0	7.0	7.0	10.0	8.0	10.0	8.0	8.0	10.0	30.0	40.0	50.0
Invoices (25%)	50	2.3	6.6	1.5	7.5	7.5	1.0	0.5	7.6	6.5	1.0	5.5	2.5
ALL SALES	250	14.3	13.6	8.5	17.5	15.5	11.0	8.5	15.6	16.5	31.0	45.5	52.5
Gross profit	78.5	4.5	4.0	2.7	5.2	4.5	3.6	2.8	45	4.9	10.2	14.6	17.1
Percentage	31.4%												

Model C

£000	*Total*	*Jan*	*Feb*	*Mar*	*Apr*	*May*	*June*	*July*	*Aug*	*Sept*	*Oct*	*Nov*	*Dec*
Cash (31%)	200	12.0	7.0	7.0	10.0	8.0	10.0	8.0	8.0	10.0	30.0	40.0	50.0
Invoices (23%)	50	2.3	6.6	1.5	7.5	7.5	1.0	0.5	7.6	6.5	1.0	5.5	2.5
ALL SALES	250	14.3	13.6	8.5	17.5	15.5	11.0	8.5	15.6	16.5	31.0	45.5	52.5
Gross profit	73.5	4.2	3.7	2.5	4.8	4.2	3.3	2.6	4.2	4.6	9.5	13.7	16.1
Percentage	29.4%												

Model D

£000	*Total*	*Jan*	*Feb*	*Mar*	*Apr*	*May*	*June*	*July*	*Aug*	*Sept*	*Oct*	*Nov*	*Dec*
Cash (35%)	250	15.0	8.7	8.8	12.5	10.0	12.5	10.0	10.0	12.5	37.5	50.0	62.5
Invoices	0	0.0	0.0	0.0	0.0	0.0	0.0	0.0	0.0	0.0	0.0	0.0	0.0
ALL SALES	250	15.0	8.7	8.8	12.5	10.0	12.5	10.0	10.0	12.5	37.5	50.0	62.5
Gross profit	87.5	5.3	3.0	3.1	4.4	3.5	4.4	3.5	3.5	4.4	13.1	17.5	21.9
Percentage	35.0%												

The bracketed percentages refer to the gross margins on cash and invoice sales. Thus, in Model A, the gross margin on cash sales is £70 000 (35% of £200 000) plus £12 500 (25% of £50 000) – £82 500 altogether.

Notes

These four examples show what happens when the same amount of annual income is traded differently – there is a range of £14 000 between the highest and lowest margins earned in these figures!

Model A shows cash sales achieved from high-margin books, with every effort being made to reduce low-margin items, and a concentration on paperback ranges which earn perhaps 40%. Invoiced sales are to libraries and companies, with little or no low-margin school business.

Model B shows a year with less concern about margins on cash sales, possibly a bookshop spending a lot of time and money getting in special orders. There is a 2% loss of margin – £4000 – though invoiced sales are the same as in Model A.

Model C is the poorest performer of all: cash sales are drawn from special orders and low-margin stock, with apparently too little effort on selling high-margin paperbacks. The invoice business is conducted at a low margin as well, with perhaps too much going to schools at a discount. As a result, the difference between this shop and Model A is £9000.

Model D is the star performer. The manager has aimed for high-margin sales, and cash only. He has not diluted profit and effort with invoiced sales at all, and this also saved stationery and delivery costs. No cash flow problems with late-paying customers – but stock control and buying has got to be good. The result is clear.

of purchasing could be 5% below that figure. On the small bookshop annual turnover we are using, 5% represents £12 500. Look at the variable margin figures on p. 46 to see what happens when different profit margins apply to the same business. It pays to watch the pennies.

Shrinkage

This term applies to the effect on gross profit of losses of stock by theft, unnoticed invoice shortages, incorrect pricing and other stock control errors. Nationally, the retail figure for shrinkage runs at about 2.5%, and every business should budget for this kind of shortage until the year-end audit proves the point one way or another.

Stocktaking

Stocktaking is an annual chore which must be done in order to place a value on stock, fixtures and fittings at a single point in the year. This is the starting-point for the audit, which theoretically works to prove that stocktaking figure and in practice finds the inevitable errors and shortages, as well as discovering any mishandling of the accounts which may be involved.

Ledgers

Computer packages follow the same principle as manual accounting, with 'ledgers' for income and expenditure. The ability to check company balances with the bank statement, and VAT, income tax and payroll features are included. The better systems provide for error-trapping, and can show the company liabilities and assets on screen as required.

If the shop uses a manual system, the accountant will advise on the style of ledger to be kept, because he will need to be familiar with the record-keeping so that audits and reviews can be effective. Not only can untidy accounting lead to errors, lost papers due to misfiling and cumulations of inaccurate information, but the accounting cost of correcting these errors at the year-end can be considerable.

Methods of Payment

The daily sales figures are the basic ingredient of the accounts and are recorded accurately as the takings are banked.

Cheques need to conform to the limits and regulations issued by the banks, but are basically guaranteed if under £50 in value. Large cheques should be verified before they are accepted or goods parted with. Since this risk lies at the till, it is important that all staff, however junior, are aware of the procedure for taking cheques. European or traveller's cheques need verifying against Eurocheque cards and/or passports, where these arise.

Credit cards are in daily use in most shops, and your service isn't complete without offering to accept them. However, the cost of doing so has to be carefully monitored, since the monthly charge may be as high as 6% (American Express), but more often around 4.5%. As the volume of trading rises, so the rates with the individual card companies and banks can be negotiated downwards, but here the individual transaction size is an important factor. There is little reduction, if any, for high volumes of turnover consisting of small amounts, say below an average of about £9 per transaction. Clearly, the cost of handling small transactions is higher for the card company. It is worth keeping a note of the trend in credit card sales, and being particularly aware of the cost to the gross profit.

Set against the costs of credit card servicing is the benefit of being able to bank the sales vouchers in the same way as cheques, with immediate effect on your bank balance.

Book tokens will also be included, but are not cash and will need to be recorded separately. Issued by Book Tokens Ltd (see p. 166), these cards with value stamps affixed are purchased in one shop and exchanged in another. Their purpose is to create a sale when a customer does not know which book to buy as a gift. The margin on these tokens is less than that on a book, and is effectively shared between the issuing and receiving bookseller. Book Tokens Ltd account for these tokens on a quarterly basis. Where more tokens have been exchanged than sold, then a refund of the balance is claimed by the exchanging bookseller; where more tokens are sold by the issuing bookseller he must pay the difference. (See Appendix 4.)

Inevitably there will be mistakes in till-keeping and these must be accurately recorded. Discrepancies should even out, but continuing 'overs' and 'unders' each day need to be investigated – there may be a staff security problem. £5 per day, small enough in a large department, still amounts to £1500 in a trading year.

Sales invoices issued to institutional or account customers are numbered and filed numerically, and are important accounting documents which will be checked at the annual audit. Careful filing is important, and needs to be thought out before a system is set up: although the computer may record figures, all the paper documentation needs to be accessible and in recognisable order.

Offering credit to a customer by giving him an invoice instead of asking for cash may be a much more important step than it seems. If such sales take a long time to be settled, or invoices are continually issued for small amounts, the costs of issuing and collection may outweigh the benefits to be gained. If a regular system of invoicing is set up then statements must be issued monthly, and a separate control of your debtors is necessary. Should you be fortunate enough to build up an invoice trade which is, say, a third of your whole yearly turnover, then the speed of payment must be watched to ensure that your money isn't tied up altogether in the spiral of buying goods in and receiving payment for them long after you have paid for them yourself.

For individuals, it is now much more effective to ask for payment by credit card. For companies, some assurances are needed that the bills will be met, and within an agreed period, usually 30 days. This will mean in theory that a bill given or sent to a customer for, say, £100 on 5th August will be due at the end of the month – a delay of 26 days at the very least. The real payment period is likely to be twice as long, because companies, institutions and local authorities will expect to pay towards the end of the month following the date of the invoice. The total of 7 weeks or more will add to your overdraft and bank costs. So the company business should be worth your while in expected volumes before it is taken on. It is normal to ask for some credit references to be given, so that you can check with companies who are already supplying your intended customer; asking for their bank means that your own bank can discreetly check on your behalf that there are adequate funds to meet your expected level of sales.

There will always be a company who does not pay, or who loses the invoice you have sent, and this involves chasing payment or sending a copy of the missing document. If the goods are claimed to be faulty in some way, then payment of the whole invoice may be held up because of one item which is damaged. These are not extreme examples and only a few instances of such claims add up to quite a headache, and an expense.

As an example, if one invoice for £100 is not paid and the money cannot be recovered, it will take a further sale of £300 to make up for the loss you have incurred, presuming that you work to a margin of about 30%.

The use of company credit cards is growing, but they are only likely to be used for small individual purchases.

A system of credit invoices should also be set up, so that errors can be formally corrected. It is bad practice simply to alter an incorrect invoice, or destroy it.

Incoming invoices

The purchasing side of your business will work as a mirror of the supply side. The bulk of your incoming documents will be suppliers' invoices, checked against the books you receive. If this job is given to staff, it will be essential both to see that training is thorough and to monitor your system regularly. Invoices which are poorly checked may mean wrong prices on your stock or an incorrect discount on the invoice; there may be shortages in the amount supplied, or the wrong book is supplied altogether. Just a 1% error rate during the year in our average £250 000 shop means a loss of £2500.

As invoices are checked they should be dated and signed as correct, and filed for entry into the manual or computer ledger system. Credit notes may be received to cover errors, or to cancel supplier invoices raised in error, and these should be verified in the same way.

Monthly, you will receive each supplier's statement of the invoices sent to you that month. Your payment method can be based on:

a) checking your invoices against this statement and paying those you have received, or
b) paying for the invoices which you have on file, without reconciling to the statement.

The former method means you don't miss any invoices, and run into correspondence with your supplier; the latter method involves less paperwork, though you need to issue a remittance advice so that your supplier knows which invoices you are paying.

Your initial credit period will have been notified by your supplier when you opened your account, but will usually be 30 days from the end of the month in which the invoice was issued (publishers may be more generous when supplying a new shop with initial stock). It is entirely proper to negotiate longer payment periods with your main suppliers, as your volume of purchases rises and for large volumes it is desirable to do so because your investment with them may be considerable.

It is also entirely legitimate to delay payment of invoices issued at the end of a month but not received until several days into the next month. As an example, a publisher may send you £100 worth of books on an invoice dated the 27th of the month, but you probably won't receive these until the 7th of the following month. In this case you have a much shorter credit period because of the delivery interval, and payment of this invoice at the end of the month following receipt puts things back in balance.

Returns

Returns are a problem. In the publishing industry with the huge variety of titles available, the returns system has become an unwieldy buffer between the purchaser and the volume of his stock.

In theory, books which have not sold in the first 3 months or so may be returned to the publisher if he agrees to accept them back for credit. They must be in good condition or a surcharge may be made, or they may be sent back to you as unacceptable. Popular and mass market paperbacks are ordered and returned on the general basis that volume purchase and display is necessary to maximise sales, a system usually agreed between the representative and the shopbuyer.

In reality, the mass of returns is proving a growing embarrassment to publishers generally, and the system encourages over-ordering by the bookseller. Books to be returned for credit have already 'died' on the shelf and will wait further for permission to return them to the supplier. Then they risk damage in transit, and the resulting credit note may take a month or more to reach the bookseller.

So it makes sense to keep this costly and negative process in check, and the bookshop's accounting system should ensure not only that stock control is as tight as can be, but that the least amount of money possible lies in the no-man's-land between returning the book and using the credit note against your next payment to the supplier.

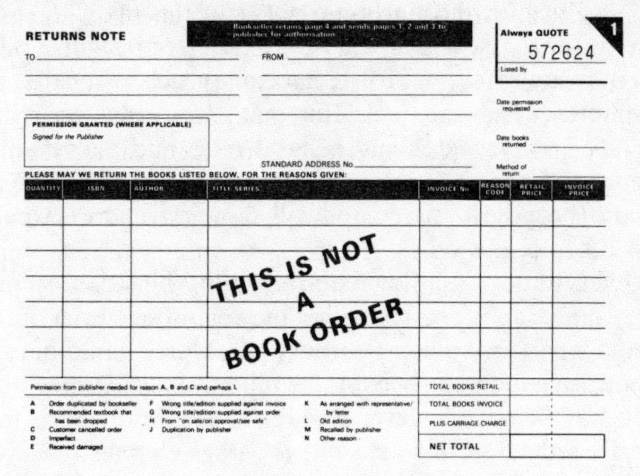

RETURNS NOTE

Bookseller retains page 4 and sends pages 1, 2 and 3 to publisher for authorisation

Always QUOTE 572624

Listed by

1

TO

FROM

PERMISSION GRANTED (WHERE APPLICABLE)

Signed for the Publisher

STANDARD ADDRESS No

Date permission requested

Date books returned

Method of return

PLEASE MAY WE RETURN THE BOOKS LISTED BELOW, FOR THE REASONS GIVEN:

QUANTITY	ISBN	AUTHOR	TITLE SERIES	INVOICE No	REASON CODE	RETAIL PRICE	INVOICE PRICE

THIS IS NOT A BOOK ORDER

Permission from publisher needed for reason A, B and C and perhaps L

A Order duplicated by bookseller
B Recommended textbook that has been dropped
C Customer cancelled order
D Imperfect
E Received damaged
F Wrong title/edition supplied against invoice
G Wrong title/edition supplied against order
H From "on sale/on approval/see safe"
J Duplication by publisher
K As arranged with representative/by letter
L Old edition
M Recalled by publisher
N Other reason

TOTAL BOOKS RETAIL

TOTAL BOOKS INVOICE

PLUS CARRIAGE CHARGE

NET TOTAL

Fig. 6 An official returns note.

Expenses

These range from regular salaries to petty cash for coffee and milk. Nevertheless, all are subject to scrutiny and must be kept in order throughout the year.

The salaries or wages paid out by the bookshop will be subject to tax and National Insurance, and some form of pension arrangement will also apply. The Wages Inspectorate may require access to salary records, because minimum salaries apply and must be maintained. Income tax payments are made monthly, direct by the employer, and records must be kept.

VAT does not apply to books in terms of an addition to the retail price. But as *zero-rated* items they must be reported as VATable sales, along with any true VAT items such as stationery and giftware, on which tax is both collectable by the bookseller and repayable to HM Customs, who are responsible for VAT.

The reporting and payment of VAT can be dealt with on a

monthly or quarterly basis. For those who have just started a business, where VAT on fixtures and fittings is reclaimable, it may be wise to arrange monthly settlement, so that quite large sums are reclaimable soon after being spent. In addition, especially for manually accounted businesses, paperwork is lessened and cash-flow improved where the assessment is monthly. The literature on VAT is extensive, but the handouts produced by Customs and Excise are usually sufficiently helpful. There are heavy penalties for those who do not treat this tax with respect!

Many business expenses will be a matter of irregular bills (on which, in many cases, VAT is reclaimable) such as repairs, advertising, motor costs and fuel. But many are only too regular – phone, electricity, water and general rates and above all, rent. Payments of these can be built into a budget, even where amounts may vary (because past records will show a trend of expense at various times of the year).

For even better cash-flow control, utility bills can be paid by monthly direct debit, so spreading the cost of essential outgoings and reducing their impact. February and March can otherwise be very expensive months, as domestic bill-payers will know only too well. It may be wise to have a water meter fitted, since this can drastically reduce fresh water and sewerage charges.

Petty cash is the bane of any manager's life, and therefore the accountant's. It is very often out of balance, and runs out just when a small amount is needed for stamps or coffee, so it is worth keeping a firm hand on the little tin box. Otherwise, the effort needed to re-balance an errant cashbook is quite out of proportion to the importance of the money involved.

Bank Overdraft and Loans

When the bookshop is first started up, a programme of expected cash-flow and a budget for the first 1–3 years will be an essential of the approach to your bank. On these figures the initial amount of a loan will be decided, and this will probably be treated quite separately from the actual overdraft.

A loan to cover the initial capital costs of setting up the business – including fixtures, fittings and lease costs as well as the start-up book stock – will be repayable over a period of time, perhaps five years. This sum and the interest payable will be calculated, and monthly repayments set up on a standing order basis. In addition, an overdraft facility will be made available, again determined by the budgets and cash flow projections. This is because the capital sum will only start up the business – it won't propel the business along. During the first year there will be more outgoings than income from sales, simply because the volume of business will not be sufficient to begin with, unless you are very lucky.

Careful calculation of the capital cost can keep the initial loan to an acceptable figure. Only prudent cash management can keep the overdraft at a comfortable level. We have already dealt with the collection of money owed to the business, and money owed by it. Buying too much stock or taking on expensive advertising, extra staff or equipment is bound to add to the level of day-to-day borrowing by the business, which is what an overdraft is.

The bank will expect the business to know what its level of borrowing is on a daily basis, because a maximum will have been agreed. Punitive extra charges may be made on unauthorised further borrowings. If the overdraft is itself overdrawn on too many occasions, the credibility of the original figures may be questioned, and the bank manager will want to know why the business appears to be in difficulties.

A review programme will have been agreed – perhaps quarterly when the business starts, annually when it is established. A fee will be payable each time a new level is agreed, even though it may be a repeat of the current figure.

It is a good idea to keep in regular touch with your local bank manager – if he understands your business and your problems, he will be more ready to help when you need him.

Computerisation

We have mentioned elsewhere in this book that a desk-top computer can make life much easier for the small business. It is well worth while discussing the various available software programs with your accountant – larger firms often have a consultant who can advise, free of charge.

Payroll, purchases, sales, VAT and income tax can be controlled through a main program, and the production of payslips, remittance advices, invoices, VAT summaries and tax payments can all be produced on demand. The manual management of these features can completely over-run a small business owner or manager, and valuable sales-creating time is wasted because the demands of such paperwork are overwhelming.

Credit Arrangements and Cash Flow

The time it takes to receive payment from a customer is vital to the survival of any business. Cash over the counter may seem very immediate, but the book being purchased may have been in stock for weeks or months, and long after the shop itself has paid for it. Stock control at its best will keep such a delay to a minimum, but success is not guaranteed.

Basic credit periods are 30 days from the date of statement, which is usually received in the first few days of each month. That is, any book received during the month of January, whether on the 1st or the 31st, will require payment on 28 February. (When a new business starts up, it may be possible to gain a longer than usual credit period from the supplier). You may be lucky and sell your supplies before the February deadline, in which case you have money in the bank. But the likelihood is that many books will take much longer to sell, and your money will be in your supplier's bank. This, basically, is cash flow (see example on p.67).

An easy manipulation of this problem is to ensure that orders are placed so that books arrive at the beginning of the month, giving a longer period of sale before payment needs to be made. Using a wholesaler to supply books very quickly (often in 3 days compared with 15 or 20 from the publisher) can mean quick sales on special orders or very popular books.

Established shops will negotiate with their suppliers for longer periods of credit, either at particular points of the year or throughout the year. A University bookseller will buy his stock at the beginning of July for student purchase in October, and will negotiate an extension of his normal period to cover the long gap in between. A High Street bookseller may negotiate longer payment on his Christmas stock, which he will want to receive in September and October. Periods of 60 and 90 days after the end of the month of invoice are not uncommon.

Such manipulation of payment terms is very necessary in such a cash-hungry business. Stock which is not bought early for seasonal peaks may not be available closer to the time. Small traders may not have the money – or the overdraft facility – to pay for stock well ahead of time, but without the right books sales will not materialise when expected. Suppliers will be accommodating in these circumstances providing the eventual payment times are kept to.

The converse of controlling payments *out* is the pursuit of payments *in*: just as the bookseller wants to delay payment until the best moment for his own cash flow, his customers will be controlling their payments in the same way. The problem may be that the business has large accounts, where several thousand pounds are tied up in books supplied to libraries, schools or a company during any given month. If the books have to be paid for before payment is made to the bookseller, then the cash flow problem is made a good deal worse. Perhaps only a few days are involved, but bank charges will still be imposed.

The best arrangement is obviously one where the bookseller has arranged longer periods of payment than the terms he has extended to his own customers. Still, the customers will need to be reminded and chased for money owed. Where once booksellers feared that strict control would send customers elsewhere for their books, the practice now is to look after the business first, and expect customers to understand that cash flow is a natural concern for any business.

5

Setting up a Bookshop

If the idea of starting your own bookshop is beginning to firm up, the next stage is to look at all the areas and considerations which need investigation before any final – and irrevocable – decision is made.

The broad headings are:

The type and style of shop
Market research
Creating a budget
Engaging a solicitor and an accountant
Locating a retail site
Seeking finance
Negotiating with landlord or council
Fitting out
Staff
Countdown to opening
Stock
Franchising

The Type and Style of Shop

Before doing any market research, you will be deciding what sort of bookshop you want to run. Whether you are thinking of a general range of subjects, or concentrating on a specialist area, there is a huge range of books to choose from – 560 000 in print at any one time – and some 61 000 are added each year. A general shop stocking everyday subjects like gardening, cookery, do-it-yourself, reference, travel and so on must rely very heavily on the buying skills of its owner to compete with any chain bookshop competition there may be locally. If your shop is merely going to repeat what can be found elsewhere in the vicinity, then your profile must be very high to establish a separate reputation. If you do not specialise completely within a specific range of subjects, you will at least need to go into greater depth and range in some of the subjects where you have competition from local traders. In recent years a number of specialist shops have grown from very specific areas of interest; film and drama, ballet and dance, biographies, and sport are examples, as well as the less specific but nevertheless interesting bargain and remainder bookshops. But you will need to have a good deal of specialist knowledge if your customers are not to see you as an amateur with no depth of understanding of the subject you stock.

A specialist shop may have a lot going for it if the subjects are interesting to a wide range of people. Thus a nautical or biographical bookshop may have a lot of casual buyers as well as a regular clientele who will go there for specialist books. But don't make the mistake of thinking that because you are keen on the subject, a lot of other people must be. If the shop is too specialist then the range of books will be narrow and even regular shoppers will be limited by what is available. Specialist shops will need to build up a mailing list so that interested shoppers who cannot always call in will receive lists of new books. Overseas visitors can hear from you long after a single visit.

The shop will need to have a positive image and an attractive range of books which change regularly to keep it in the public eye. In a general shop, it will not be sufficient simply for you to be nicer to customers than seems to be the case in a chain bookshop; the ambience of the premises, the approachability of yourself and the staff will be all-important, and you will find yourself specially ordering all the books which other traders have preferred not to deal with, or have not been competent at obtaining.

Types of Bookselling

Whilst it would not strictly be true to say that there are as many different kinds of bookselling operations as there are types of books, you should be aware that there are a great variety of methods of book retailing: from the health food store or garden centre with a rack of books and magazines by the till, to the vast academic bookstore servicing the requirements of universities and libraries; books reach the general public today via many channels.

Let's look at a few of the most easily identifiable.

The Academic Bookseller

Academic bookshops exist to provide books and services primarily to educational institutions and their students, and also to other academic organisations and bodies which may be connected to universities, e.g. libraries, research groups, etc.

The academic bookseller needs to maintain close liaison with the university or college tutors, in order to establish which texts will be required by both staff and students, and in what quantities. Such a shop may need to provide services such as making sample copies available, export facilities for overseas institutions, and library supply. Some academic booksellers also serve the more general needs of the local population, with some cross-over of their markets (e.g. students buying popular or gift books, the local townspeople purchasing textbooks.)

Because of this an academic shop's sale pattern may show peaks at key times in the academic year (i.e. September/October) and also at the more generally popular book-buying times such as Christmas. Academic bookshops usually require some of their staff to have educational qualifications in certain specialist areas.

Library Supply

Most public and institutional commercial libraries purchase their book stock via a mixture of ordinary bookshops and specialist library suppliers: libraries which buy books at a discount through the library licence system will usually have more than one name appearing on their licence, in order to give them the opportunity to 'shop around' and make use of different booksellers' services.

However, supplying books to libraries can be a very sophisticated operation, depending on the specific requirements of the library customer. Booksellers are generally expected to supply books ready jacketed in protective covers, with tickets, and with a variety of cataloguing work already completed on behalf of the library (e.g. accession numbering via a bar code labeller). Libraries today tend to use very technologically advanced systems for information storage and retrieval and for electronic communication, and it is important that the library bookseller has a grasp of this if he is to do well in this area of the book trade. Some general High Street booksellers handle only a small amount of library business, whilst other booksellers deal exclusively with libraries.

Specialist Booksellers

Apart from those booksellers whose stock is geared to minority interest groups, such as train spotters or ornithologists, probably the two biggest areas of specialisation in bookselling (apart from those previously described) are children's and religious bookselling.

Both require a special kind of dedication to the market from the bookseller; it is likely that you will need to take stock to exhibitions, meetings and gatherings if you are to cultivate potential customers, and obviously the greater depth of knowledge of the subject you can demonstrate the better. Religious and children's booksellers need to maintain close links with the clergy and teachers, in order to keep abreast of trends in thinking in both areas, and therefore most booksellers of this type are likely to find themselves involved socially as well as commercially with their customers at some stage or another.

As with booksellers selling books in other well defined specialist areas, shop sales can be augmented by mail order, where specially selected potential customers are targeted. With the rise of the chains and multiples in High Street bookselling, it has been suggested that specialist or 'niche' bookselling could be the salvation of the small independent.

The High Street Bookshop

There is a huge variety of shops in this category, ranging from the tiny one-man owner-occupier business to the large bookselling chains. Whatever their size, High Street shops have one thing in common: it is their function to determine the needs and desires of their local market, and to stock and sell accordingly in the face of competition from the other types of retailer who are all jostling for the pound in the public pocket.

High Street bookshops may therefore concentrate on the best-sellers, which they know they can sell, or stock a wider range to capture the interests of a wider market. This latter course of action is obviously more of a gamble, and this is where bookselling skills are needed to make this a risk worth taking. These shops are often referred to as stock-holding bookshops, as opposed to CTNs, newsagents and others.

CTNs (Confectioners, Tobacconists and Newsagents) account for approximately 14% of book sales in the UK. They will usually stock only a narrow range of bestsellers, which will probably have been supplied and merchandised by a wholesaler (thus removing to some extent the bookselling skills of stock selection and stock control).

Many other outlets are now stocking books on subjects relating to their merchandise – we have already mentioned health-food shops and garden centres. To a certain extent, the appearance of books in these outlets can be said to be beneficial to the stock-holding bookseller, as customers who may not be able to find all their requirements on a book-rack in the garden centre may then visit their local bookshop for a wider selection and more informed service.

Books are also sold in yet another way in stores other than those already mentioned, that is, in department stores and stationers with book departments. W H Smith can claim the largest share of UK book sales in retail terms, and yet they are perceived by most people to be a stationers, record store and newsagent as well as a bookseller. Many book departments in large stores will offer a range equal to that of the good, stock-holding High Street bookseller, and will offer the same range of services, such as special orders for customers, school or library supply, etc.

School Suppliers

School suppliers, like academic booksellers, tend to work very closely with their customers (i.e. teachers and schools). Much of the business is done on a contract basis, with bookshops submitting tenders for school supply contracts at the beginning of the financial year. This is because many of the books sold will be non-net titles (see p. 9), and may be discounted, so booksellers will be competing on both a service and price basis.

As with library supply, some High Street bookshops are involved with supplying local schools, whilst other businesses exist solely to sell to educational establishments. Some of these may not operate through normal bookshop retail premises, but may run a showroom where teachers can come and examine books and discuss their needs. Obviously, as with library supply, such bookshops will employ a higher percentage of 'behind the scenes' staff, such as packers, clerks and accounts staff, as opposed to shop-floor booksellers.

Other areas of bookselling include mail order and export. Again, many existing bookshops may conduct some mail order or overseas business, but specialists do exist.

Export bookselling requires establishing contacts with overseas institutions and customers, and may involve one person in the company travelling abroad to set up contracts. Often, export booksellers work with the British Council, which runs schemes for book provision overseas, and a detailed knowledge of legislation concerning both the financial and customer requirements of export is required.

Mail order bookselling is somewhat more difficult to describe, as it appears in many different guises: at its simplest, it is an operation selling specialist interest titles to a list of known devotees of a subject, and at its more complex, it could be a major book club selling a wide range of titles at a discount (see p. 139 for an explanation of book club regulations). Whilst mail order bookselling does not really fall within the scope of this book, it is as well to know of its existence, and be aware that it can encourage people to visit bookshops who may not normally do so, in search of a wider choice.

Having looked briefly at the variety of types of bookselling activity, it will be up to you to choose which area interests you most. It is obviously important that if you opt for a specialist area, you should choose a subject about which you are knowledgeable, and for which you are certain there is a market. General High Street bookselling will obviously offer the widest range of experience for someone starting out in the trade, although there are pros and cons attached to working in either a large or small shop. In a small shop, you can expect to learn everything about bookselling from unloading delivery lorries to running the accounts and making buying decisions, but you may not encounter such a wide variety of customers (individual, institutional or corporate) or be able to learn about particularly sophisticated systems. In a large shop, you may be able to learn about a subject area in great depth, develop knowledge of bookshop technology, etc., but you may find you are somewhat departmentalised and do not see the whole bookselling process from start to finish. If you are working for somebody else in the book trade, there is always the option of changing jobs in order to broaden your experience or find an area which suits you better; if you are starting your own bookselling business, there is obviously more onus on you to make the right choice first time!

Market Research

This entails finding out all you can about the town or city where you intend to trade; if you haven't decided on a location, the work will need to include all the likely conurbations* in an area or county. It is wise to avoid locating in your own town or city just because it is convenient, though it may prove that your neighbourhood can support a bookshop. Your final decision must be made for sound commercial reasons, and not just for your own comfort.

If you decide on a shortlist of places to investigate, you will need to look at the possible competition you would have in each place. Are there already well-established book outlets which would be difficult to compete with? It isn't sufficient merely to have confidence in beating an established bookshop. There must be plenty of scope for further outlets, or a definite weakness in the present competition which you can exploit. The only available local shop may look run down, untidy and unattractive, and you will feel able to do better. But it is also worth remembering that an established business does not lose its custom overnight. What has taken a long time to build up can take quite a time to fade away, too.

How large is the population? Do they all shop in your chosen area, or is there a town or city nearby which is also a strong attraction? What plans are there to expand or develop local shopping facilities – can you take advantage of any of these? Likely

*A conurbation is the area surrounding a town or city which tends to use that town or city as its main shopping place and social venue. A conurbation can stretch for a good way and will include rural communities. One conurbation may be close to another, and the relative strength of the city centres will be important to you.

developments could make difficulties for present trading areas. New shopping centres or large building developments can change trading habits for a long time, and sometimes for good.

What is the quality of the other types of trading in the town – will your own shop be well integrated in the community? Well-to-do areas with a good sprinkling of luxury shops may already have bookshops, but would provide a good book-browsing clientele. Rough and ready market areas may look very busy and thriving, but will provide few actual book buyers.

Small towns and villages can very seldom support a bookshop which provides a dependable living. There may be existing shops which have developed a good trade over a period of time, particularly if they have established a mail order list, but starting a new shop in these circumstances flies in the face of today's established shopping habits. Friends may be thrilled at your suggestion but friendly encouragement will not be enough, even if they remain regular users of your bookshop.

So the clear possibility is that you will have to move house, or be prepared to commute some distance, if you are to set up a viable business selling books. There is the obvious short-cut of buying an existing concern where you would like to trade. This is entirely possible but it is best to do all the market research anyway; you may well find the reasons for the run-down state of the business on which you have been keeping an eye. To approach a business before this spadework has been done means that you run the risk of being persuaded by a specific proposal rather than your general findings about the ability of the location to support a good business.

Creating a Budget

Any budget must start with the level of turnover you expect to achieve in a year, especially the first year. An example budget is shown on p. 66 The income of the business provides the means to meet your everyday costs, your own personal income, and your trading profit. Therefore the sales budget must be approached realistically, since it is only the owner who can make the turnover happen, and sales growth can only come from the confidence of the person in the driving seat. It is no use constructing a sales budget simply to make all the other figures work, or to convince

An example annual budget

	Totals £	Jan £	Feb £	Mar £	Apr £	May £	June £	July £	Aug £	Sept £	Oct £	Nov £	Dec £
CASH	200000	12000	7000	7000	10000	8000	10000	8000	8000	10000	30000	40000	50000
INVOICES	50000	2300	6700	1500	7500	7500	1000	500	7500	6500	1000	5500	2500
ALL SALES	250000	14300	13700	8500	17500	15500	11000	8500	15500	16500	31000	45500	52500
GROSS PROFIT 29.8%	74500	4295	3845	2545	4975	4355	3350	2605	4355	4725	9550	13775	16125
Property	16000	1333	1333	1333	1333	1333	1333	1333	1333	1333	1333	1333	1333
Salaries	31000	2583	2583	2583	2583	2583	2583	2583	2583	2583	2583	2583	2583
Post/print	2900	242	242	242	242	242	242	242	242	242	242	242	242
Phone	1000	83	83	83	83	83	83	83	83	83	83	83	83
Motor	1000	83	83	83	83	83	83	83	83	83	83	83	83
Finance	7600	633	633	633	633	633	633	633	633	633	633	633	633
Other	7050	588	588	588	588	588	588	588	588	588	588	588	588
ALL EXPENSES	66550	5546	5546	5546	5546	5546	5546	5546	5546	5546	5546	5546	5546
NET PROFIT	7950	−1251	−1701	−3001	−571	−1191	−2196	−2941	−1191	−821	4004	8229	10579

The Gross Profit figure is reached by calculating cash sales as earning 31%, and invoiced sales earning only 25%, because of their possibly specialist nature. The resulting annual percentage of gross sales is 29.8%, although this varies from month to month because cash and invoice sales change in proportion to each other.
NB: All figures have been rounded for simplicity of demonstration.
Key: *Property* includes rent and rates, *Salaries* includes all pay, tax and NI. *Post/print* includes all stamps, carriage, stationery and bags. *Phone* includes rent, calls, etc. *Motor* includes fuel, service, tax. *Finance* includes audit fees, bank charges, depreciation. *Other* totals cleaning, repairs, computer, subscriptions, advertising and petty cash.

Cash flow example

	Totals £	*Jan* £	*Feb* £	*Mar* £	*Apr* £	*May* £	*June* £	*July* £	*Aug* £	*Sept* £	*Oct* £	*Nov* £	*Dec* £
1 Cash Income	200000	12000	7000	7000	10000	8000	10000	8000	8000	10000	30000	40000	50000
2 Invoices paid	50000	2300	6700	1500	7500	7500	1000	500	7600	6500	1000	5500	2500
3 Total Income	250000	14300	13700	8500	17500	15500	11000	8500	15500	16500	3100	45500	52500
4 Creditors		−28752	−9405	−6555	−9855	−8025	−11145	−12525	−6270	−5895	−12525	−25575	−28350
5 Expenses		−5546	−5546	−5546	−5546	−5546	−5546	−5546	−5546	−5546	−5546	−5546	−5546
6 + Depreciation		250	250	250	250	250	250	250	250	250	250	250	250
7 Previous balance		5000											
8 Flow month		−14721	−1001	−3351	2349	2179	−5441	−9321	3934	5309	13179	14629	18854
9 Cumulative	[−12338]	−14721	−15722	−19073	−16724	−14545	−19986	−29307	−25373	−20064	−6885	7744	26598

This model illustrates what happens to the amount of cash available to the bookshop month by month.

Line 1 is the monthly cash taken over the counter. Line 2 is the payment of invoices customers have received with their goods, and presumes that in general this will be a month later than the issue of the invoice. Line 3 is the total monthly result of these two incomes. Line 4 shows the monthly payment to suppliers,and presumes that these payments will go out a month after the goods were received. Line 5 is a regular average of the cost of overheads – staff, rent, telephone, etc. Of course, in practice the figures will vary from month to month. Line 6 adds back the figure for depreciation, normally part of the expenses total. This is because, although depreciation is part of the management accounts, it is not paid out in cash, since it represents an allocation over a period of time of the amount already spent on capital goods. Line 7 is an assumed balance at the start of the year – in this case there was £5000 in the bank on 1st January. Line 8 shows the result of adding up income, subtracting creditors and expenses from that total, *for the month in question*. Line 9 shows the result of starting the year with £5000, and subtracting or adding each monthly result. The running effect can be seen at any month of the year.

The bracketed figure of £12 338 is the average overdraft for the year. Naturally, the figures will change if sales differ, invoicing varies or expenses peak. Similarly, if customers pay their accounts late, or the shop pays its suppliers late, the figures can be quite different.

Whilst this set of figures shows a healthy trend, it can be seen that in fact only the December peak in sales brings in the results. In January, payments to creditors and expenses will bring the bank balance back into overdraft again.

second and third parties that you need a certain level of loan. It is also fatal to turn to further loans to help prop up a business which is not making ends meet.

As a rule of thumb, your total annual turnover will need to be eight times the salary bill you expect to support, but this will provide a modest living only. Thus for two people, one as owner earning £10 000 p.a. and one as assistant earning £5000 p.a., with an added approximate 20% for tax and National Insurance costs, totalling £18 000, the turnover indicator is £144 000. In turn this means you must be able to take nearly £2800 per week over the counter, or £460 per day, including Saturday. Two people running a six day shop at this level will find life pretty tough going with small reward.

For this reason the model shop indicates a turnover requirement of about £250 000. The turnover is sufficient to generate a small profit, trading is reasonably comfortable with the number of staff involved, and there is some room for sales generation – the manager is free some of the time to visit customers. The two people running the £144 000 example were 'earning' £72 000 each in sales during the trading year. Whilst this is much higher than industry averages – £50 000 per year is more normal – the level is not quite as high as it may sound. Much of the business will happen around Christmas time, when some part-time extra help can be employed. The real drawback of such a small turnover is the restriction on both people, who must spend a great deal of their time in the shop, day in and day out, with no day off or time to break the routine.

The £250 000 model is earning about £50 000 per head of staff per year, though with some extra help from a Saturday assistant. Holidays will still be an awkward time, but the summer is often quiet from the trading point of view (depending on the locality).

Where are the Customers Coming From?

If this simplistic turnover calculation is extended to a mythical example town of 25 000 population – only about half of whom will be regular earners – then *every one* of these earners must spend £15 per year in your shop to support your turnover. Such regular and loyal custom is hard-won and certainly not immediate. It is more likely that conurbations of 75 000 and greater will be needed to support both your idea of a starting turnover and later growth.

The Budget Format: Capital and Revenue Expenditure

The proposal for a new business will need to look at money in two ways: firstly, the initial lump sum with which to start the business, itself divided into two parts – set-up costs ('fixed capital'), and initial book stock ('working capital'). Secondly, the annual costs of running the business, from the rent to the petty cash.

Fixed Capital

Your fixed capital budget will be the amount you expect to spend on the shop and its fitting-out before you begin trading, and the mechanical equipment you will need, e.g. till, computer, etc. You'll need to make an exhaustive list of the capital items to ensure you haven't forgotten an expensive piece of equipment. They should include the following, which are either self-explanatory or are items which are discussed more fully later in this chapter (marked thus*):

Lease purchase ('key money')*
Legal costs of rent agreement, etc.*
Shop front (redecoration or replacement)*
Interior decoration
Shopfitting – shelves, island units, etc.*
Carpet or flooring
Lighting
Statutory kitchen and toilet facilities
Shop sign and section indicators
Counter
Till, microfiche, computer
Telephone installation
Possible security measures*

The sums involved will depend on your choice of site, shopfitter, equipment and so on. The list needs to be determined early on, because the eventual total sum will be a crucial feature in whether or not you go ahead with your proposal, and indeed whether or not you get a loan at all.

Lease purchase – 'key money'

You may well be required to pay a substantial sum of money to take over the lease of the shop you eventually decide to have. £10 000 would be quite possible, and perhaps much more, depending on its location and proximity to other important traders. An extreme example is that you would have to pay a great deal of money to be next door to Marks and Spencer (and would face stiff competition!), but a lot less if you took a site in a side street several hundred yards from the city centre.

The price of a lease is the amount an occupier expects to receive in consideration of the value of the site, *if you are taking it over during the currency of an existing lease*. Thus, if you were to take up a property which had three years to go on its existing lease of seven years, the present trader would calculate the difference between the existing rent and what could be gained if the property were re-let at a current market rental. Of course you will need to be sure why the existing tenant wants to give up; make sure there are no local reasons why he wants to get out, and which may be equally disadvantageous to you.

A landlord may also take the same line by allowing a new trader into a site at the existing rent, but demanding a calculated premium on the remainder of the lease. He might alternatively offer an entirely new lease at a higher annual rent. The actual calculations may in the event not be so sophisticated – simply a premium which is the price the ex-trader or landlord believes could be gained from the site.

Legal costs

There will be costs involved with taking over an old lease or starting a new one, and the incoming tenant is usually expected to pay the landlord's costs in drawing up whatever agreement is necessary. Your solicitor will advise on the various clauses which may be involved in the lease agreement, and his fees also will be payable.

Shop front

You may have found perfectly good premises, but with an inappropriate shop front, or in a state of disrepair. Although an expensive prospect it may be best to provide a new one; at the very least the existing structure may need thorough redecoration. The shop front is after all your greatest physical asset as far as new customers are concerned.

Shopfitting
The cost of fitting out the interior of the shop will depend on the size of the premises and their condition, and the quality of finish you expect from your shopfitter. A minimum figure of £30 per square foot should provide good quality shelving, carpets, lighting, displays and counter.

Security measures
The property you find may be perfectly secure in terms of strong front and rear doors, and adequate rear window protection. If it is not, you should consider replacing any weak doors, strengthening window protection (bars at the rear, for instance), and providing security locks which are approved by your property insurer.

Working Capital
The money you will use to buy your opening stock is part of your initial loan, and will be calculated on the basis of what stock is required to back up the budgeted sales in the first year. Our model shop expects to have a £250 000 turnover with a 4:1 stock turn, meaning that, on average, a quarter of the turnover will be in stock at any one time – £62 500 at retail prices or about £40 000 at cost.

Expenses will often have to be paid out even when sales are low, and there may not be enough in the company account to cover everything at once. Extra cash may also be needed for higher levels of stock over short periods, or for slow-paying account custom. These fluctuations are normally dealt with by using an overdraft at a level agreed with the bank. For the size of business we are talking about, this may be in the region of £15 000. A fee of about £150 per annum for this level of overdraft will be payable, and the bank manager may prefer to review the overdraft quarterly at first, rather than every year.

Before we leave the subject of capital, let's see what figures have now accumulated! The following table gives sums which might well mount up when planning the model bookshop we have used as an example throughout this book:

		£	
1	Lease	10 000	
	Legal costs	1 500	
2	Shopfitting	30 000	(1 000 sq. ft. × £30)
	Shopfront	3 000	
	Other equipment	4 000	
3	Opening stock	40 000	
	TOTAL	88 500	

You may think this is a daunting sum, and in many ways it is, because most of it will be spent forever – in the event of failure, only a fraction of the stock might be recouped. Your financial commitment is total, so your personal commitment and drive need to be absolutely behind your project.

It is true that you can start a bookshop for far less than the figures given – you may not pay for a lease at all, your fitting costs may be smaller and your stock not so large, but the results will be smaller too, perhaps less attractive, and may not provide the impetus to keep you going at the required level.

Revenue

Revenue expenditure is the money spent during a year on day-to-day costs, using the revenue or cash received from sales.

The layout on pages 74–5 shows the sort of costs involved in the Charter Survey results for 1988–9, assuming the middle-size bookshop is under consideration. The Charter Survey is produced by the Booksellers Association from members' annual returns, and shows average spending in the various cost headings by bookshops up and down the country. The averages shown are a good indicator of what you can expect to spend in the various cost areas, but of course you can control some of this spending either from the start or during the year, as was shown in the chapter on accounting.

Some of these costs will be determined by the location and size of the premises you have in mind. A large city centre site is going to command a high rent, high rates, and several staff because it should be busy, particularly at lunchtimes and on Saturdays. In a smaller town site, these costs will be lower, but so will the turnover.

We have already looked at the sort of figure you might need for your own salary, and only you will know if this is sufficient. Almost certainly you will begin by earning far less than you have been used to, and your personal outgoings should be carefully assessed to see if a lower income can be tolerated.

These are the main headings of other expenses you will have to consider:

1 Salaries other than your own
2 Tax, insurance and pensions arrangements
3 Rent
4 Business Tax and water rates
5 Electricity, perhaps gas
6 Telephone
7 Postage, packing and carriage
8 Stationery – bags and letterheads
9 Advertising
10 Repair and maintenance of equipment and premises
11 Cleaning
12 Insurance (of premises and stock)
13 Petty cash
14 Possible vehicle costs
15 Depreciation
16 Bank charges – overdraft and loan costs
17 Audit and accountancy fees
18 Subscriptions
19 Teleordering and computing costs

Items 15 to 19 require some explanation

15 Depreciation This is the capital cost of items which have a life longer than the current year of trading, such as shelving, carpets, lighting, typewriters, desks and so on. Although the items themselves will have been bought and paid for in the first place, the annual accounts bear a share of their cost over a period of time; this allows the business to be judged on the true cost of all its constituent parts year by year.

Thus, if £30 000 has been spent on these capital items and they are judged to have a 10-year life, the annual accounts will bear a charge of £3000. In reality depreciation is more complex, with different items bearing different periods of depreciation, and is

Sales and business ratios by size of outlet by profitability

BOOK SALES	SMALL Below £155,000			SMALL/MEDIUM £155,000-£232,000			MEDIUM £232,000-£330,000			MEDIUM/LARGE £330,000-£525,000			LARGE £525,000-£1,000,000			SUPER LARGE £1,000,000 or over		
Net Profit Category	*Low*	*Ave.*	High	Low	*Ave.*	High	Low	*Ave.*	High	Low	*Ave.*	High	Low	*Ave.*	High	Low	*Ave.*	High
Number in category	10	*10*	14	7	*12*	15	12	*12*	15	12	*14*	12	10	*12*	15	8	*10*	10
SALES RATIOS																		
New book sales%	88.1	*76.2*	77.4	78.5	*88.1*	77.5	91.3	*86.4*	89.3	91.8	*96.2*	87.4	93.3	*78.7*	90.6	74.0	*95.9*	87.8
*(a) Retail	91.5	*79.9*	82.5	92.4	*89.2*	90.2	85.6	*83.7*	89.8	78.2	*80.7*	90.1	80.5	*74.9*	95.1	82.1	*80.1*	97.0
*(b) Library	1.3	*4.5*	2.8	2.2	*4.2*	2.0	4.0	*5.7*	3.5	5.4	*7.6*	8.1	11.1	*9.7*	2.0	4.7	*18.8*	2.9
*(c) Book Agents	5.2	*5.2*	0.9	0.3	*0*	0	0.7	*3.4*	1.4	1.3	*0.3*	0.1	0.1	*0.9*	2.3	1.4	*0*	0.1
*(d) Schools	2.0	*10.4*	13.8	5.1	*6.0*	7.8	9.7	*7.2*	4.3	15.1	*11.4*	1.7	8.3	*14.5*	0.6	11.8	*1.1*	0
Other good sales%	11.9	*23.8*	22.6	21.5	*11.9*	22.5	8.7	*13.6*	10.7	8.2	*3.8*	12.6	6.7	*21.3*	9.4	*26.0*	*4.1*	12.2
PROFIT × COST RATIOS																		
Gross Profit %	29.3	*30.0*	33.7	24.7	*29.0*	32.8	32.2	*30.4*	31.7	28.8	*27.6*	33.2	26.6	*28.5*	38.1	28.1	*28.1*	34.9
Total Expenses %	38.2	*28.8*	26.5	33.7	*29.2*	26.4	34.6	*25.6*	22.0	31.4	*24.7*	24.1	29.4	*25.3*	28.5	29.5	*22.6*	22.1
(a)Wages and salaries	17.3	*15.5*	13.7	17.5	*16.6*	14.7	16.1	*13.6*	12.3	15.0	*14.0*	13.5	14.6	*15.7*	13.5	16.5	*14.0*	12.5
(b) Rent and rates	6.5	*5.5*	3.7	4.7	*5.3*	4.9	6.1	*4.6*	3.2	7.3	*3.9*	4.8	5.6	*2.8*	7.9	3.4	*2.4*	4.0
(c) Other working expenses	14.4	*7.8*	9.1	11.5	*7.3*	6.8	12.4	*7.4*	6.5	9.1	*6.8*	5.8	9.2	*6.8*	7.1	9.6	*6.2*	5.6
Net (trading) profit %	(8.9)	*0.2*	7.2	(9.0)	*(0.2)*	6.4	(2.4)	*4.8*	9.7	(2.6)	*2.9*	9.1	(2.8)	3.2	9.6	(1.4)	*5.5*	12.8
OPERATING RATIOS																		
Stock turn (books)	2.6	*3.7*	2.5	3.4	*3.5*	3.1	3.1	*4.0*	3.4	4.8	*4.7*	3.2	3.3	*3.6*	2.8	3.3	*3.6*	2.8
% by which retail stock written down to cost or valuation	36.0	*42.*	42.0	33.0	*37.*	39.0	39.0	*37.0*	40.0	42.0	*38.0*	41.0	42.0	*38.0*	41.0	40.0	*42.0*	41.0
Sales per person employed (£)	41200	*44200*	41000	58000	*54600*	50800	56900	*57600*	74000	53700	*57800*	56100	55500	*57500*	58900	75300	*76200*	74700
Sales per sq. ft. (£)	122	*147*	151	181	*194*	146	163	*208*	235	191	*268*	157	190	*272*	190	293	*330*	276
DETAILED COST RATIOS																		
Wages, salaries, NHI of staff %	12.1	*8.2*	7.7	10.6	*9.1*	11.2	11.6	*9.7*	8.4	10.7	*9.6*	13.0	11.8	*11.2*	12.1	11.4	*12.5*	11.7
Pension contributions for staff (other than NHI) %	0.6	*0*	0.2	0.2	*0*	0.1	0.2	*0.1*	0.1	0.1	*0.4*	0.3	0.5	*0.5*	0.7	0.3	*0.4*	0.3
Working directors' and proprietors' basic salaries and NHI only %	4.5	*0.6*	4.1	6.5	*6.8*	3.2	3.6	*3.2*	3.2	3.8	*3.3*	0.2	1.7	*3.3*	0.6	4.5	*1.1*	0.4
Pension contributions to directors and proprietors																		

(other than NHI)%	0.1	*0.7*	1.7	0.2	*0.7*	0.2	0.7	*0.7*	0.6	0.4	*0.7*	0	0.6	*0.7*	0.1	0.3	*0*	0.1
Rent %	4.5	*3.9*	2.6	3.5	*3.8*	3.5	4.1	*3.0*	2.2	5.4	*2.9*	3.1	4.2	*1.9*	6.5	2.4	*1.5*	2.8
Rates (incl. water & sewerage) %	2.0	*1.6*	1.1	1.2	*1.5*	1.4	2.0	*1.6*	1.0	1.9	*1.0*	1.7	1.4	*0.9*	1.4	1.0	*0.9*	1.2
Gas, electricity %	0.9	*0.5*	0.5	0.5	*0.4*	0.4	0.5	*0.5*	0.4	0.5	*0.4*	0.6	0.5	*0.4*	0.5	*0.4*	0.4	
Telephone %	0.7	*0.6*	0.4	0.4	*0.6*	0.4	0.4	*0.7*	0.4	0.5	*0.4*	0.2	0.4	*0.3*	0.3	0.3	*0.3*	0.3
Postage and carriage charges %	0.7	*0.4*	0.8	0.7	*0.6*	0.5	0.7	*0.6*	0.6	0.6	0.5	*0.7*	0.5	1.5	*0.6*	0.5	0.8	*0.8*
Printing and stationery%	0.4	*0.4*	0.6	0.7	*0.3*	0.4	0.5	*0.4*	0.4	0.5	*0.4*	0.4	0.6	*0.4*	0.3	0.5	*0.5*	0.3
Publicity and advertising %	0.5	*0.5*	0.5	0.3	*0.4*	0.3	1.2	*0.4*	0.5	0.6	*0.5*	0.3	0.7	*0.7*	0.5	0.8	*0.6*	0.4
Repairs, renewals & maintenance %	0.5	*0.4*	0.4	0.6	*0.4*	0.6	1.1	*1.5*	1.4	0.4	*0.4*	0.3	0.3	*0.5*	0.4	1.5	*0.5*	0.6
Vehicle running & travelling costs %	1.3	*1.2*	0.7	1.3	*0.8*	0.4	0.5	*0.7*	0.4	0.7	*0.5*	0.2	0.5	*0.5*	0.2	0.4	*0.3*	0.1
Interest paid %	1.9	*1.8*	1.5	2.1	*1.2*	0.7	1.2	*0.5*	0.9	0.7	*0.8*	0.1	0.9	*0.7*	0.2	0.6	*0.3*	0
Bank charges (excl. interest), audit and accountancy %	2.7	*0.8*	0.5	0.9	*0.5*	0.4	0.6	*0.6*	0.4	0.5	*0.5*	0.4	0.3	*0.3*	0.2	0.5	*0.4*	0.1
all working expenses (excl. depreciation) %	3.0	*0.4*	2.3	2.1	*0.9*	3.6	4.1	*0.4*	0.4	2.7	*1.6*	1.9	3.4	*2.1*	2.2	2.6	*0.5*	1.9
Depreciation & write-offs	1.8	*0.8*	0.9	1.9	*1.2*	1.0	1.6	*1.1*	0.7	1.5	*0.6*	0.9	1.1	*0.7*	1.8	1.1	*0.7*	1.0

Averages are used for statistical reasons

Copyright The Booksellers Association 1990

Note: This table, taken from the 1988/89 Charter Group Economic Survey, analyses the performance of single Booksellers arranged according to size and profitability. Examination of this Table confirms that it is Booksellers in the larger categories who manage to achieve the best performance in terms of stockturn and employee and space efficiency ratios.

While the spread of gross profit in all size categories is very consistent there is quite a remarkable range of total expenses in all but the two largest categories. The fact that this matches a similar spread of net profits is ample testimony that control of overheads is the key to greater profitability.

an area best dealt with in more depth by your accountant when the time comes.

16 Bank charges The bank will charge you interest on your initial capital loan – this interest will be part of the monthly repayment you make as a standing order. There will also be charges for every cheque paid out, and credits paid in to the business. There are further charges for the cost of the working overdraft which you will have agreed with the bank before you begin trading. These charges appear on your bank statement at quarterly intervals, and are based on the trading levels and cash movements of that quarter.

17 Accountancy and audit fees Your accountant will make a charge for the annual audit of your accounts; for our model business, this will be between £1500 and £2000, though much will depend on the tidiness and 'accountability' of your book-keeping.

It could well be worthwhile – unless you have a payroll package on your computer system – for your accountant to calculate and inform you about the monthly salary bill, per individual employed. He will certainly have a computer and the task will be an easy and relatively cheap one. Beyond that, and certainly in the early days of a business, you will want his advice on a range of financial matters, for which he will make a charge.

18 Subscriptions This covers the annual fees payable for three of the most likely costs you will encounter: the subscription to *The Bookseller*, paid for annually; the annual subscription to the Bookseller's Association, a fee based on a minimum turnover, beyond which the rate is adjusted on a turnover scale; and the annual subscription to *Whitaker's Books in Print*, either on microfiche or as published volumes.

19 Teleordering and computer costs Strictly speaking, Teleordering – the overnight electronic system of transmitting daily orders – is a subscription, since an annual fee is involved. But this fee, along with a probable maintenance fee, is substantial enough to be accounted for separately. In addition, a computer system will have a maintenance agreement of its own which will be renewed annually.

Engaging an Accountant and a Solicitor

You may not be happy with the figures, and in any case you do need to discuss your calculations with someone, so now is the time to look for an accountant if you don't already have one. He will tell you that apart from the sales figures – which in the end only you can be confident about – and the expenses figures, you will need to assess what your cash flow will be for at least the first year.

As discussed in the Accounting chapter, cash flow is vital to the survival and future of the business. Initially, the bank will want to know what your cash demands are going to be. How this can fluctuate from month to month and from one year end to another is demonstrated in the cash flow table on page 67, which is discussed fully in the Accounting chapter.

It is normal to set up a trading plan which covers the first three years of your intended business, including sales, expenses and cash needs. The budget can be extended from the first year's detail by adding percentages of growth in all figures, based on anticipated inflationary factors for expenses and realistic growth as far as the sales figures are concerned.

Although you do not need a solicitor at this particular point, it might be wise to make sure that you have one standing by so that you can move ahead when you are ready. He will be needed for setting up the lease ownership or agreement when you find premises, and if he practises in the town, he will have local knowledge of problems which may affect you.

Locating a Retail Site

From the budget you have created, you can calculate the size of premises you need, and will get from this an indication of likely rent and rates costs.

The Charter Survey on pages 74–5 shows that sales per square foot is an important measure of the worth of a bookshop. Premises trading from around 1000 square feet of selling space and selling £250 000 per year will be earning £250 per square foot, which would be a very good figure for the sort of shop we are considering. The difficulty will be that no shop premises are ideal from every point of view, and a balance must be struck between these main requirements:

Proximity to pedestrian shopping routes
Size of shop in relation to fitting costs
Appearance of frontage
Basic facilities
Rent and rates
Possible repair needs
Length of lease

Before considering these headings from your point of view, it is worth spending a short while on the subject of estate agents, who have an unfortunate reputation as far as domestic house-buying is concerned. You will need to approach two or three local firms, with a fairly clear idea of the sort of premises you require.

You should specify the size of premises you need, and be firm about the minimum and maximum areas you can consider; state clearly that ground floor is essential. If you can afford to renovate older premises, or can only contemplate ready-to-trade sites, say so. You may be able to specify the area in which you want to trade, because you know the locality well. It would be as well to say that you won't want to trade within so many yards of your competitors, or that you don't mind being quite close to them. You should list the facilities that you would find ideal, such as rear-entry goods doors, installed kitchen and toilets, existing lighting, up-to-date electrical wiring and plumbing and good decorative order.

Estate agents usually have a commercial office, besides their house sales department, and will be able to tell you how easy or difficult your task is going to be in the area. They can also indicate the sort of price you will have to pay in rent, rates and premiums.

Besides a premium on the rent (described further in the section on landlords), there may be a premium on existing fixtures and fittings in the premises which you are offered. It is rare to find such fittings useful for bookselling, unless they are very basic items like flooring and lighting. Even so, they may not be what you would have chosen, and if taken up may dictate your layout and design scheme more than you would like. It will not usually jeopardise any agreement to reject these offers, unless the site you have chosen is an especially 'prime' one, in which case other bidders for the site may take the fixtures offer as part of the overall cost of getting the premises they want, and you would have to follow suit to keep in the running.

As with house sales, your estate agent will be charging the landlord with the cost of finding a tenant, and you should not have to pay any fee. Of course this does mean that the agent is not working in your interests, but will be keen to get the best deal from an incoming tenant. It really is a case of 'buyer beware' and any site you choose should be fully inspected for sound structure, and any agreements scrutinised by your solicitor, who *is* acting in your interests because you are paying his fee!

Do not rely on the estate agent for a steady flow of information about sites: he will need constant nagging if the new shop is to be set up at your pace.

Shopping Routes

Good premises in the wrong location are almost always a disaster, sooner or later. Potential customers must be able to find you easily, or be able to visit you during their normal shopping runs. It may be tempting to justify good premises in a quiet location, particularly if the rent is comfortable, but the outcome in sales will be disappointing and possibly disastrous.

If a site seems to be a good one, then you need to judge how many customers you could expect to see on a given day. There is no substitute for standing in the vicinity and counting the hourly rate of passers-by: on a good day, on a rainy day, on a weekday, on a Saturday. If you need a good comparison, spend an equal amount of time outside a good central location which is trading. If you counted 300 people an hour passing the local department store, and your site managed about 100 an hour, you would begin to get a feel for how many people you might actually attract *into* the shop.

How Big a Shop?

A large shop at an acceptable rent in a good position may at first sight seem a good proposition: but remember that you must pay for the fitting out, and unless you plan to trade from only a percentage of the premises in the first instance, such opportunities need careful thought before you go ahead.

Appearance of the Frontage

A plain, modern glass front will demand a good window display all the time, or a particularly attractive internal layout with effective lighting. An old-fashioned frontage may repay good refurbishment, and reappear in new paint as a very attractive asset. You may, however, find that the old shopfront needs to come out because it is inappropriate or in need of too much repair, and replacement can be very expensive. The shopfront obviously affects the customer's first impression of your business.

Basic Facilities

We have covered these in earlier paragraphs, but the obvious needs to be restated. What is the power supply and is it safe? Is there effective heating, and by what means? Is there a toilet and washing facilities, with hot water, and are they all in good condition? Are there adequate locks on the front and back doors and windows? What is the condition of the decorations, flooring (what is underneath the carpet?) and plumbing? Are the ceilings in good order and if lights are installed, are these safe and usable? Is there a water meter? Is the power supply shared with another tenant in the building? Is there a telephone line installed?

Rent and Rates

These we have discussed in terms of your own budget, but you will need to check with other retailers in the area to see if there have been any difficulties in the past with rent increases or reviews, and the council services for which the rates pay. It will be a way of meeting possible future trading neighbours, to go in and ask them about their experience. Most people will be very helpful.

Possible Repairs

Obvious features such as woodwork, walls, partitions, stairs and other fixed structures should be inspected to ensure that only decorative attention is needed, unless you are prepared for structural changes. But here the lease needs special attention, because there may be a clause which binds you to repair the exterior as well as the interior of the building. This could be a very onerous undertaking, and unless you are considering a substantial building for the long term, such clauses are best argued out of any new agreement with a landlord.

Length of Lease

In the section on dealing with the landlord, the question of taking over the remainder of a lease is covered. But you will also need to know how long any fresh lease can last, and whether you have the option to renew that lease once the period is over. It will be very damaging to build up a good business only to find that you are obliged to hand back the premises to the landlord, perhaps because he has a long-standing agreement to sell the property for development.

Seeking Finance

Once you have finalised your calculations and analysed your figures sufficiently to decide how much money you will need, you will have to approach your bank. Before you do that your figures must have been organised on paper in a recognisable way, which your accountant can help you with. If the bank is to be your source of income, the manager can help you too, but it is better to go to him with a plan which looks organised and competent; you have to convince him that you are able to invest this amount of money, control it, and develop the business profitably. Seven out of ten businesses fail quite soon after start-up, because there isn't enough money to carry on, or the idea wasn't good enough, or because insufficient expertise has been put into its development. These simple points will be very much in the bank manager's mind!

The figures should be presented from two points of view: a profit and loss estimate for the first year at least, and preferably the first three; and the cash flow which would result from the business running on these lines. A business uses cash to keep going, and to run out of cash when things are going well can be even more devastating than if things are going badly. The Table on page 67 illustrates cash flow, and should be seen alongside the profit and loss table for the same business.

If your figures are acceptable, the bank will advance your money in two ways; by straightforward loan for the main costs of setting up the shop (fittings, lease costs, legal costs, etc.), and an overdraft facility, which is determined by the cash flow forecast you have provided. You can then draw from your facility as necessary, and as the demands of the business change from week to week and season to season.

Negotiating with the Landlord

Presuming that you have located a site, you will need to negotiate with the landlord of the premises, who may already have set a rent. The landlord may be the local council. Either way, you will need a solicitor to help you study the lease, its implications for you and the business, and to ensure that you do not take on any onerous clauses. In a standard lease of, say, seven years, there may be a rental period of four years at so much, and a second period subject to an increased rent to be determined when the time comes. Longer leases may have longer and/or more frequent rental periods.

The Uniform Business Rate will, of course, be determined by the local authority, and water and sewerage rates will also apply. It will almost certainly be much cheaper to install a water meter from the very start, rather than pay according to the rateable value of the premises.

A rent-free period can often be arranged, meaning that you can enter and install yourself on the premises for a pre-determined period without paying rent; the period may be as much as six months, more likely two or three months, though of course it may not take you nearly as long to get ready for trading.

Fitting Out

How you spend your money on shopfitting will be a matter of thinking through the style of bookshop you want to project. Lighting, colour, shelving style and material, floor finishes in tile or carpet, shopfront and display space all have important roles in the final effect. The quantity of books you will stock and the way they are displayed (and therefore sold) will be dictated by this original design and the thinking that goes with it.

To control the cost of the shopfitting and the layout of the shop, you will first need to draw a floor-plan layout of the retail space you intend to use. If you have an area measuring, say, 30 feet deep and 20 feet across, you will want to keep an area at the back of the shop for unpacking, storage of essentials like bags, vacuum cleaner, etc., and if not already installed, kitchen and toilet facilities. Once these have been allowed for, the remaining space needs to be used to maximum effect if every part is to be profitable.

Layout will be simpler if you have just the ground floor area to fit out. If you do have upper or lower floor areas to fit as well, then you must be careful to site book sections and subjects to suit their position in the building. For instance, it is unhelpful to put children's books in the basement or upstairs, because many of your potential sales come from mothers with young children and prams or pushchairs, for whom stairs will be a major obstacle. Posters, stationery, bargain books and popular books for younger readers are well suited to lower and first floor areas because they are attractive items for people who don't see staircases as a barrier.

The distance between shelves is important for browsing – narrow aisles mean people cannot look at lower shelves without constant interruption from passers-by; wheelchairs and pushchairs must be catered for in the same way. Four feet is the usual minimum distance between the bottom of one fixture and its neighbour.

Sight lines through the shop are essential for both the customer and the shop staff. If a shop appears cluttered or smaller than it actually is, because shelving has not been planned and sited in an open fashion, potential browsers will not come in. Impulse sales will be lost. For the shop staff there is the problem of overseeing the shop from their workpoint or the till area. Theft is as rife in bookselling as it is in other retailing. Cosy corners and hidden areas are inviting to the thief. Because of their size books are easily stolen, and regular thieves will be quite able to steal several books in one visit – and they will return several times if the shop layout is helpful to them.

Most often a shop is longer in depth than it is in width, which means a corridor effect is bound to be created by normal shelving layout. This can be broken up by staggering the central display stands either face-forward or face-sideways, so that the total effect is more interesting to the customer. The ends of sections can be shelved or grooved for book display, instead of remaining empty and unproductive.

Since 60% of the shop customers will be women, it makes sense to ensure that the top shelves of the wall sections can actually be reached! The rule is 'eye-line is the buy-line', and though slavishly following this concept would mean only three or four shelves per section, it is also true that the bottom and top shelves need to be either well-lit or the books placed face-forward if they are to be noticed at all. To put the books on a high top shelf simply because it is there is simply storing them, not selling them.

The central display stands – often called gondola or island fittings – are usually double-sided, and should be only chest-high. This allows for clear visibility through the shop, and lighting can be most effective.

Signs and lighting are probably the most important aspects of shopfitting when all is said and done. If the customer cannot see a clear section sign across the full length of the shop then the signposting is inadequate. Lettering should be clear and plain without being dull; fancy lettering in confusing colour combinations should be avoided. Sub-section signposting should only be used where absolutely necessary, e.g. 'Mediaeval History' or 'Chess' as sub-sections of History and Sport or Pastimes. This is because the sign has to be small enough to fit the edge of the shelf, resulting in a size which isn't clear at a distance.

Finally, the layout of the main display area, or several small display areas if the shop has sufficient space, should be open and accessible; a table in a corner simply to fill that corner is not displaying the books to their best advantage. Books which are displayed in the window should be easily found in the shop, or the impulse which brought the customer in will be lost. Displays in the shop should have a theme, or single titles should be strongly presented in stacks with a supporting poster or display. Presentation of new or popular titles needs to be much stronger than may seem necessary: a customer with only a few minutes to spare at lunch-time or just before you close may be ready to buy, but only if the books are clearly to be seen.

Shelving will be constructed of wood-veneered chipboard or metal: both can be made up in a wide variety of grain finishes or colours. Whilst wooden shelving is often the most sympathetic material, metal can be coloured in striking ways, and will often be cheaper to buy. Shelving fixed on channels which are screwed into the wall are less expensive than free-standing units, and this is an important point to remember when first inspecting the premises. Walls in poor condition needn't be shelved direct, but strong and therefore expensive units are needed to stand clear of them.

The principal shopfitting companies* can give you a full planning and layout service included in the overall contract price, and will be able to propose a number of features which will probably not occur to the newcomer to bookselling. It will naturally be cheaper to stick to the standard design of unit supplied by the shopfitter, with small adaptations where necessary; specially designed fittings are usually expensive, and can be disappointing in practical use.

Staff

Staff need careful recruitment, particularly since their future is tied to your own in new and untried circumstances. An advert in the local paper at least three months before opening is necessary to ensure that you have time to choose staff, allow them to give up to a month's notice to their present employer, and have them start work before the opening.

New staff, whatever their previous background, will need training, and this should be done before the immediate run-up to opening, when all hands will be needed for the job.

People with previous bookselling experience may not be available, so applicants with general retail experience are the next best thing. You'll need people who are used to customers and routine shop tasks. If you are taking on several new people, they should meet beforehand to allocate tasks for immediate work, and the long term.

The best approach is to write out the tasks which you expect to be done by others on a daily basis, and list these in order of importance as a job description. This will help order your own thoughts, and explain the job to applicants at interview. If you expect jobs to have different levels of responsibility, then priorities need sorting out so that the right people are taken on to do the relevant tasks. In a large shop, an assistant manager will have an overall view of other staff jobs, as well as having his own specific jobs to do.

Employees are rightly protected in many ways by employment

*(see the classified adverts at the back of *The Bookseller*)

law, and you should familiarise yourself with the main concerns in this field. Ignorance of issues which could affect your staff may lead to damaging and time-consuming problems which will divert you from the business in hand.

Broadly, legislation controls the hours and conditions of work, minimum pay rates, sex and race discrimination, sick pay and unfair dismissal. Since the whole area of employment legislation is a book (at least!) in itself, it is worth discussing the main principles with your solicitor at an early stage.

It is stating the obvious to point out that staff fairly treated and reasonably paid will usually respond with a good commitment to the business. But people working together in close and often trying circumstances will lose their tempers at least once in the trading year. There will always be someone that works better and harder than another; always someone to whom the accidents happen, or who is often ill; always someone who finds it difficult to keep good time; and there is always the possibility of someone who is dishonest in some way. Security firms say that 50% of the stock losses in retailing can be put down to staff pilferage.

For these reasons, you will at some time be required to make fair judgements, or be a disciplinarian or a sympathetic listener when you have least time to give to the problem in hand. Other people are demanding.

It is prudent to keep staff records, including name and date of birth, address, phone number, next of kin and their phone number, salary when starting and at each review, together with a brief note of any developments of difficulties which might have later relevance. Though it may seem bureaucratic, it is worth setting aside an hour every six or twelve months for staff to be appraised: to be told their good points, where they can improve, and for you to listen to what they have to say about their work and how the job is going.

Countdown to Opening

At this point you should organise a very clear timetable leading up to your opening date, and even for a short while afterwards. Staff will need to be employed, accounts opened with suppliers, membership of the Booksellers Association set up (see pp. 144–153), supplies ordered, received and shelved. Advertising must be arranged, contacts made with the local press and any societies and organisations you think may be interested in what you are doing, especially if you are setting up a specialist bookshop.

If you are taking on staff, you must be familiar with the basics of employment law and what the likely costs will be, including basic hourly and weekly pay for your area and the type of job you are offering, the payment of tax and national insurance.

You will need to register for VAT, even though books are zero-rated; cards and stationery are subject to VAT. With the advent of a barrier-free Europe, it is increasingly likely that some level of VAT will eventually apply to books, too. Here it is best to register for monthly statements rather than quarterly, at least initially, so that you can quickly recoup the VAT you pay out on setting-up costs – important to cash flow!

If you are buying a computer and using accounts and stock control packages, you must allow time to get used to the program methods, and set up any supporting manual systems accordingly.

All these points and more will need to be carefully phased if you are to accomplish everything in reasonable time, especially if you are organising the new business with little or no help. All the factors which depend on others will need to be checked and re-checked – the promised start date for shopfitters may need to be preceded by electricians and decorators; staff will need to start early enough for training, and to be able to help you set up shop; nothing can start if you do not have possession of the premises on the promised day. You may not need a Filofax before opening day, but you will certainly understand why others use them!

Stock

The cost of your stock will again depend on your expectations for sales in the first year: in the table on p. 66 we talk of £250 000. With an expected stock turn of 4 in the year, this would require a start-up stock with a retail value of £62 500. This is high, even considering that you will pay only about 67% of this at cost – £42 000. It is better to start at a considerably lower level, because you can build your stock quite quickly after the shop opens. As trading carries on, you can see what stock sells best and order accordingly. A large commitment to stock before you open may leave you with a lot of titles which do not sell as you hoped.

For the table, we have used an opening stock of only £25 000, costing you just under £17 000.

The importance of choosing the right stock cannot be overstressed: odd books or incomplete subject sections will look very awkward on opening day. Routine stock must be accurately and efficiently replaced if the range is to remain competitive and effective.

The backlist range available from UK publishers comprises all the titles which are still in print, and which may have been available for years. A bookshop which restricts itself to simply replacing successful choices from its own past records will be ignoring a rich vein of titles which will have some measure of sale and, more particularly, will add variety to the stock range. The great majority of books published enjoy a relatively short period of success, and then fall into the backlist hinterland.

Such a huge variety of books means that many customers will not see a fraction of what is available and with care, the selective bookseller can refresh his stock in an attractive way by ranging through previously published titles.

A word of caution about buying in fresh stock: there is no need to buy *any* stock which does not afford the best margins available. It is bad economics to buy books because they are considered 'good stock', despite the fact that they carry poor discount terms. It is entirely possible to create a good stock range from suppliers who recognise that generous discounts are crucial to profitable trading. (See also pp. 46–7 for information on margins.)

Discounts

Trading margins can vary widely from supplier to supplier, depending on the quantities which are ordered and the total price of the consignment in question. To both newcomers and established booksellers, the resulting confusion makes little sense.

Book pricing is the job of the publisher, who may well not assess the price of the finished product until quite late in the production process. Books of general interest, for sale in the High Street and to public libraries, usually provide the standard best discount of 35% on the retail price. These may include both hardback and paperback titles, principally fiction.

Many books are academic or scholarly in content, and have less sales potential. Since fewer copies are printed, the price rises – production costs are necessarily spread over a small number of books. Publishers often offer lower discounts on such titles as they will be promoting directly to colleges and institutions and therefore speculation on the part of the bookseller is arguably less than on more general titles. Keeping one or two copies of such academic titles in stock at key times of the year could result in the sale of 40 or 50 copies when the book is adopted for a course.

Given that these lower discounts range between 20% and 30%, the bookseller must be careful when stocking such titles. If the publisher's promotional costs are higher, it is also true that the bookseller must invest in perhaps expensive textbooks, and will need to promote his stockholding to potential student purchasers. What he is unable to sell he may return, but without careful stock control – and good liaison with the local college or university who recommend the books – these returns can be expensive.

Allied to this market are school books, which are normally expected to sell in class sets of, say, 30 or so. The same arguments regarding low discounts and the reasons for them apply. There are companies who specialise in the supply of books to schools and libraries, whose volume sales and purchasing allow them to negotiate better terms.

Since supply costs – storage, invoicing, packing and distribution – are high, there is usually a minimum supply level below which the publisher will not fill an order, or will impose a handling charge. This will apply to paperback orders where the overall invoice value is low, unless a reasonable volume is being sent; or to the sale of expensive books where one or two copies only are bought.

Visits from suppliers' representatives are pretty frequent in the bookseller's calendar, and many suppliers will apply different discounts to their new books, for the reasons given. The careful buyer will always check that his purchases include only those books which earn him the best margin.

There is no reason why discounts cannot be greater than the standard terms on offer. A shop which intends to specialise will have main suppliers whose discounts should be negotiable upwards. A larger shop than our standard £250 000 example can expect to be building good annual turnovers with the main paperback publishers, and here discounts may move above the normal 35%.

Using a Wholesaler

For the new bookseller running our average to small bookshop turning over about £250 000 per year, the use of a wholesaler is really essential. Supplies of titles at this level of turnover, if controlled by a stock system which correctly indicates a 'little and often' approach to stock replenishment, will frequently be at a level which could attract small order surcharges or poor discounts. At cost price, daily ordering on this basis averages only about £500; spread over ten suppliers, this must mean regular invoices of only £50 or so. These are levels which are uneconomic to both trader and publisher.

In the past decade the concentration of principal stock lines in the hands of only four or five wholesaling companies has become a phenomenon of the change in book retailing. It is now possible to stock an entire bookshop from a single supplier – or two at most – and to do so by buying regularly and at acceptable trading margins.

Not only does this present the trader with a single source of supply for almost all his needs, but the one further great advantage is speed. Average supply times in book publishing are falling from the lamentable standards of recent times, but it still requires about two weeks (though often more) to receive books once they have been ordered. Customers don't appreciate slow service, though they may tolerate it until there is an alternative.

If you are new to bookselling altogether, then one of the principal national wholesalers will be able to help in your selection of basic stock lines. Some wholesalers will supply titles with re-order slips or computer printouts which will mean you can easily re-order titles as you need them: the titles which sell on opening day may need very quick replacement, and the speed of service from wholesalers is usually much better, across a wider variety of titles, than is the case with individual book publishers.

Since each title is peculiar to its publisher, the range of titles sold on the first day may come from many different publishers; ordering from them will be expensive and time-consuming. Minimum order levels from paperback suppliers will mean that you simply can't order some books until you have sold more. With wholesalers, most of these problems will not arise.

The best approach is to visit a branch of a multiple bookseller, to see what basic sections they have. Reference, children's, fiction, local interest, arts and crafts are obvious sections for a general bookshop, and the basic books for these can be chosen from the subject listing in the wholesaler's catalogue or warehouse. It may initially be safest to select two or even three wholesalers, visit them and compare stock range, service and terms of supply before re-visiting the one you have chosen, to place your opening order. The principal companies tend to have different approaches to the depth and range of stock which they carry, in any case.

Using a wholesaler for the initial stock will also mean you have much better control over your total value of ordering. The counter to the wholesaler argument is that you should be aware of your main publisher suppliers so that eventually you can order direct from them at improved terms, because of the size of your regular orders and eventual annual turnover. Using a wholesaler in this situation reduces or even eliminates your ability to negotiate better terms.

Credit Arrangements

When starting up a bookshop the decision can be made between taking on stock from a wholesaler who will expect payment in the usual trade period of 30 days from the end of the month following the date of the invoice; or taking stock from individual suppliers on an extended payment basis which can be up to six months for reasonable initial stock orders.

The wholesaler method must be carefully controlled; a small portion of the initial order may often be returned for credit after an agreed period if unsold, so that initial uncertainties can be allowed for, but not as a rule thereafter. But smaller quantities of stock can be taken on in the knowledge that replacements can be obtained within two or three days.

Taking stock from publishers can mean more freedom as far as returning unsold stock is concerned, and longer periods of credit are attractive. But this can lead to a lack of caution in the exuberance of starting a business, with the difficult and even insuperable outcome of too much stock, and running out of cash at an awkward time such as a busy trading period. The principle rule remains to order little and often, though care must be taken not to order such small quantities that accounting for both the supplier and bookseller is expensive and time-consuming.

If the wholesaler is reasonably nearby, there is the added benefit of taking stock on a cash and carry basis.

Franchising

There has been very little franchising in the retail book trade, despite the widespread introduction of this style of selling in other retail trades. A limited attempt has been made in the recent past, based on a wholesale warehouse, but this has ceased; a bookselling company in the UK has advertised franchising in principle, but no nationwide packages are currently available.

The accepted notion of franchising as far as a bookshop is concerned would involve a package which would be 'rented' by a trader who wished to work within the control of a company who had devised a standard shop design and layout, a stock control procedure, supply arrangements possibly based on a central supply depot; local and national promotion and advertising, and full training for all staff.

Many household names (Wimpy and Prontaprint are diverse examples) are outlets provided by a host company who sell their expertise (and often their supplies) to a franchisee who pays to 'rent' these facilities, as well as the retail site itself. If sufficient training has been given, and there is good ongoing support, this approach to retailing has much going for it.

6

Marketing and Promotion

What is Marketing?

Marketing may be defined as the organised presentation of a product to an identified customer type. In retailing generally, the major shop chains have a very clear idea of the customers they want, and what they expect those customers to want from their stores. In turn, the customer expects a range of products, in a familiar environment, presented in a certain way, often with a guarantee of service and quality.

For example, everyone knows the type of goods they might buy at Marks and Spencer, how it will be displayed, and what level of service to expect. Marketing in this respect is not simply a good selling ploy, it is absolutely essential to the profitability of the company involved. This is illustrated by the changes in the Woolworth chain which were instituted several years ago. Before then, the stores had lost their way in terms of the type of customer they wanted to attract, and in turn the customer had lost a sense of what Woolworth's stood for. Many of the stores have now been completely re-planned and people now know exactly what Woolworth's stands for; the confusion has disappeared. The results for Woolworth's were very good.

Own Brands

The High Street multiples have a clear idea of what they will buy from their suppliers, because the identity of their style and approach to their goods is reflected in the goods themselves. Suppliers must reach acceptable standards, and may often be asked to provide specific ranges of goods which are exclusive to that store alone. 'Own brands' are important to store images, but are very often provided by the manufacturer or supplier of a household-name brand; for example, Sainsbury's baked beans may well be Heinz beans in a Sainsbury wrapping. It isn't cheating! – the quality is the same, but the way it is presented is different. The customer may well only buy Sainbury's beans at Sainbury's, because he or she has become sensitive to own-branding, and will ignore Heinz baked beans elsewhere.

The customer doesn't lose; Sainsbury's don't lose – they gain a more regular customer; Heinz don't lose, because they're selling baked beans anyway.

Style

You probably wouldn't buy products from a store with an unclear or dated style – back to Woolworth's, where the past image has meant that perfectly good products were not bought because many people didn't want to use that store.

Style is the essence of presentation in a store that wants to build a regular custom. Everyone wants a bargain and you might browse and buy in cheap bargain shops, but you probably won't be *loyal* to that store and return for their products no matter what. Display, shopfront and in-store decor, staff attitude and quality of service are all essential to style.

Consistency

All these points are only worthwhile if the store is *consistent* in its approach. Marks, Woolworth's and W H Smith, would not last if they did not present the same level of marketing all the time. Once started on a certain plan, they cannot afford to let go, change course or run down, without serious consequences.

Fashion

The term doesn't just mean modern dress sense: the regular customers will have a life style of their own and this has its own fashion. Many stores aim for a type of life style and supply that sort of customer. Habitat is an example.

To do this, Habitat secures its own type of customer for the Habitat range, and the customer becomes loyal to that style of product. The bonus for Habitat comes when the 'customer base' grows; that is, more people are attracted to Habitat furniture and accessories. The situation is thus reversed: from Habitat finding a 'niche' in the market, to Habitat creating its own market.

What About Advertising, and Reputation?

Of course these can be essential, but you need something worth advertising. You must have a good 'package', and reputations must grow, not remain static. Advertising 'Come to Luvabooks' isn't enough. In the end, you can almost dispense with advertising – good marketing means the customer will go to that store anyway, regularly.

So attention to what you already do, how it can be focused and improved, comes first – with a long-term objective clearly defined.

How Does This Affect Bookselling?

All the principles we have looked at should naturally apply to retail bookselling. It is often said that bookselling is different; the product has remarkable and renewable resilience, it is fresh and ever-changing, its glamour is attractive to a great many people. But these are simply the good things going for the product, which still needs to be brought to everyone's attention.

It is as well to remember that *everyone* is a customer some of the time. Shop assistants buy goods in their lunch hour; university professors dig their gardens and need new plants at the weekends. Every customer sees better and better presentations in our High Streets, and products which are poorly displayed or under-marketed will be ignored.

An established bookseller already markets in different ways, as part of his daily and seasonal routines. Look at this list:

Window display
Special order service
In-shop displays
Specialist sections
Credit cards
Library supply
Speedy ordering
Local adverts
Signing sessions

Outside signs, fascia
Specialist staff
Company letterhead
Textbook supply

These are all daily things, and being complacent about daily things is often a problem. Well-dressed staff with clean nails, clean shoes and a good customer manner are a must. The most patient and helpful member of staff is best employed at the special order desk. The library customers will welcome a call every so often, to prove that their supplier is showing continuing interest in their regular custom.

Either the manager or his deputy should ensure that mistakes don't recur, which means finding out why they happened and stopping the problem at source. Staff may need some re-training, or there may be an error in the system. If stock control is computerised, there should be a knowledgeable assistant for the person who normally runs it. And a well-dressed window is of little use if staff are not aware of what stock is being displayed there.

There are quite a number of questions the bookseller can ask about his business, and the answers can help enormously in understanding the way the business works, and how marketing and promotion can sell more books. The following list gives some of the main pointers:

What percentage of the business is special orders? Usually special orders form about 15% of the daily sales; more than this level might indicate that stock control isn't working effectively, or that the stock range should be broadened. Maybe your service is a lot better than the competition, and should be encouraged further.

What is the average retail price of a special order? Taking small orders just to be helpful can lead to problems: such orders are rarely profitable and if you pass on surcharges to the customer, resentment will be caused. Small orders can be taken on the understanding that they will be added to the next stock order, to avoid surcharges.

If the average price is high, then you may have a clear indication of a specialist market you can expand. People who are prepared to pay high prices for their special orders usually have a special interest which can be developed into a shop section, or even be catalogued. These customers can be advised when new books in their field are due to be published.

How long does it take to get a book for a customer? If your average ordering time isn't anything to write home about, then you need to take action, otherwise you will be antagonising customers who can get their orders elsewhere. A wholesaler may be the answer, or more frequent unpacking and checking of incoming parcels.

How far would the shop go to get a special order? Make sure your staff know what the special order procedures are. Would you phone a supplier for an urgent order? What does 'urgent' mean? Everyone has a different level of panic for their own special needs!

Who checks the special orders to see if there is a trend you could stock for? Someone in the shop, usually the manager in a small business, should watch the special orders. Regular requests could become stock items, or highlight inadequate repeat ordering of stock.

How do regular customers react to your displays? Are your displays looked at by customers as they browse around, or are they ignored because they are not sufficiently arresting? What are the best points in your shop for displays? Have you got too few or too many?

Who complains, and why? If you get complaints, are they reasonable, and can you do something to improve things? Do your staff tell you when complaints are made?

How many people come in and don't buy, compared with those who do buy? Book trades surveys have shown that 40% of your sales may be impulse – people are buying books which they had no intention of getting when they came into the shop. If your own sales survey shows a lower figure than this, your displays or stock range may need improvement.

What is your busiest day, other than Saturday? Watching your daily takings should be an absolute habit, and watching the weekly trend of busy/quiet days can identify good days for new displays, and when to have most staff in the shop.

Your quietest day? Is there anything you can do about it, or should you leave all your chores for this day?

Your worst section, and why? Stock control or a special till analysis will tell you if a section is worth the space it is taking up. Is it because you haven't spent enough time on choosing the right books for the subject, or is one of your competitors much better in this area than you?

Your best section, and why? Why is your best section as good as it is? Could the winning principle be applied to the weaker subjects? Could the section be made to perform even better than it does?

You can't market without the answers to these questions. They all help to indicate your place in the market, and how you can improve your 'niche' in the customer's perception of your service.

Promotion

In order to promote your business effectively, you need to do much more than simply prepare an advert and keep the cost as low as possible. How you display your shop to the public, and how regularly, are vital to the customer's perception of you and your business. One-off, occasional advertising is only of use if you have a particular and short-lived title or service to offer, and even then the advert must be a prominent one. But there are several ingredients in the promotion mix:

Promotion budget

You should have some idea of your annual budget, or you will make short-term decisions about promoting the business and be unable to follow them up with effective repeat advertising. You need to decide when to place your adverts for maximum effect in the year, the month or the week.

If your budget is a substantial one, you can spread the amount over different features: newspaper ads; special promotions, perhaps a competition with a prize; author signing sessions; early evening receptions for home-going regular customers; even a literary luncheon or supper.

What sort of advert?

You may think of advertising in the local paper, a district or regional paper, on the local commercial radio, on regional TV. These aren't as expensive as you might imagine, *when you take into account the potential result.*

Get a realistic idea of the cost of an advert, and what will go into that advert. For example, a newspaper advertisement: one advert relying on a single event is quite chancy, and must be a good size to attract enough attention. If you have a good author visiting the shop for a signing session (and the publisher may well help with the cost of the advert), you have a good one-off opportunity. But the copy must be placed in a prominent position in the paper – the right-hand side of the TV page for instance. If you don't insist on a proper placement (for which you may pay more), your precious ad may appear on the sports page or worse! It will need to be at least double the size of a credit-card to make any impact. Don't leave it too late to book or you will have no choice of placing anyway. If the paper or magazine is published daily, consider the right evening of the week to advertise. Friday and Saturday are poor days for expecting the reader to look at every page and take in what is there – many people go out for the evening, and don't sit at home reading the paper. Thursday is a good day and although fewer people are now paid weekly, there is some value in attracting people when they have just been or are about to be paid.

You then have a choice to make. If the advert costs £150, you'll need to sell three times that figure just to cover the ad – will £450 be possible? Your answer may be definitely not. But your choice may be to place the advert anyway and get a lot of interest in your shop, as well as the book in question. The longer term effect may be beneficial, especially if you regularly advertise in that paper.

Regular ads

It may be better to take out a contract with the local paper, undertaking to put a certain size of ad in every week. It may seem expensive (though you will get a serial discount); but your customers will have your name in front of them every week. You can change the copy when you want and add any special events.

Radio and TV

The same rules apply to air time: you need to budget and see if the results could possibly justify the expense. There's no harm in asking your local stations for a rate card.

If you do take it further, make sure that your spread of slots reaches your customers at the *right* time. Stations offer cheap packages, but this may mean that you are talking about cookery books to truck drivers at 3 o'clock in the morning!

Your costs won't just be air-time – you will pay for studio preparation of the ad, perhaps including voice-over. All this may well be worth it – don't be put off by the seemingly huge cost. You might find a publisher or group of publishers willing to help you in a seasonal promotion of your shop. If you are good at drawing up a script, get one ready, but be prepared for criticism and suggestion from the station's advertising manager. They do know what the public will listen to, and what becomes boring. A lot of information in any advert, whether written or spoken, becomes boring to the casual reader or listener, and the speed at which radio ads are necessarily broadcast may mean that an overlong message is never properly taken in.

These are just two ways in which you can spend money and get noticed. There are others:

1 Ask your local paper to arrange a spread for you. You tell them which publishers/suppliers to contact, with an agreed contribution cost. You supply some editorial about your shop or service. They do the rest. This does have a possible drawback: it may be better to warn your intended contributors that they will be contacted by the newspaper, or their calls may be treated like any other cold-call sales talk. A further problem may be that of an overall cost of, say, £1000, your contribution may be £350. This you may accept, but the price goes up if only four out of five intended contributors actually agree to pay. You may not have time to look for a stand-in, so keep a couple of suppliers in hand, just in case.
2 Arrange an advert-backed competition, perhaps about a new book and its subject, or associated with a local cinema. You donate a small prize or prizes. The paper reports the result. The cinema may well agree to share some of the cost of the advert, or the prize.

'Free' marketing

There are some features which you can build into your annual programme of events which are free, or at least heavily subsidised to a level which makes them very worthwhile.

Successful 'opportunity' advertising or marketing relies on your knowledge of your market and your locality.

Phoning new customers

'Cold-calling' potential customers in local companies needn't be the embarrassment that it sounds. Not many people appreciate calls at home about double glazing, but companies get sales calls all the time. You can prepare the way by compiling a letter about your services, send it to half a dozen managing directors or sales directors in your locality (find out their names first so that your letters reach the right people). Then phone them up about a week later to see if you can interest them in taking books as, for instance:

1 Desk reference books
2 Training handbooks
3 Computer manuals
4 Christmas gifts instead of drink

Your letter should include details of your shop and the type of books you sell, as well as describing your service and how you can deal with special orders and professional books. It is surprising how many companies will believe that you cannot get books on a specialist subject, simply because you don't normally stock them. Many will have written to distant shops and publishers direct to get books which they believe are difficult to obtain; they could well be very pleased to find a local supplier. The letter should be direct and friendly, not formal or overstated, and shouldn't be more than a page long. Think how much of your own mail you throw in the waste-basket!

You don't have to know about specific subjects to sell books on those subjects, unless you are aiming to provide a specialist service. Be straight about your ignorance if you are asked for details. These are often available from the publisher's catalogue or you can phone them up to ask for details you need. After all, you're both in the selling game.

Other promotional ideas
Radio Reviews could be offered to the local station; you may be able to get a small slot in which you review a chosen new book. Although you are not directly advertising your bookshop, your name will become known, and you may be asked to participate in something else, perhaps an arts review. Small stations will quite often be glad to have extra material to insert in the day's programmes, and a carefully, thought-out suggestion for reviewing popular types of books – say, cookery or travel – might well catch a producer's eye.

The same applies to *newspaper reviews*; the local paper will receive review copies of books which the publisher believes may have some local interest. It is surprising how bad such random attempts by publishers to get newspaper space can turn out to be. Many books, often on minority subjects, are of little interest to the population served by the local newspaper. The reviewer often writes about a book simply because it has arrived on his desk, and the title is unlikely to sell well because it does not have sufficient local appeal. There is room here for the local bookseller to provide an interesting book for review, especially if there really is a potential local interest featured in it. The same suggestion for radio reviews applies here.

Window displays may be 'leased' to publishers, with their agreement either regularly or as one-offs. Publishers often produce professional high quality promotional material for windows, which can be very effective. You may wish to hire a window-dresser to do your windows on a regular basis. This could be partly paid for by a contribution from the publisher (although they may argue that the costs of producing the point-of-sale material for the window is contribution enough).

Even if you are unable to get contributions from suppliers, it is well worth the cost of employing an agency to send a window-dresser, say, once a month. Whilst you may gain a great sense of achievement from making up your own window displays, or a member of staff may have some talent for it, the standard of High Street windows is now so high that it is difficult for an amateur to avoid a home-made appearance. Besides, the amount of time a fair-sized window can take up is considerable, and is a hidden staff cost perhaps better directed to other work. Half a day's work from a professional will cost about £40, though there may be an extra charge if there are travel costs involved. You might get the name of a good window-dresser from a neighbouring trader, or you could suggest that two or three of you share a day's cost. The result can be stunning and worth every penny.

Signing sessions can be very lucrative, or complete failures! But they're usually free, and create interest in your shop as well as in the books being signed. At the very least, such sessions attract notice and add to the general 'background noise' you are making about your business in the area.

A local author who has written a book about the town or city or region is a focal point for a specially advertised publication day, but perhaps no more. The public will not flock to see local authors unless they have been nationally or regionally famous for previous books.

A national author who lives locally is potentially a completely different matter. He or she may be very happy to support a small local bookshop by coming along for a lunch-hour to sign copies of the book and chat to local people. Every big author lives somewhere near someone! But don't depend on interesting news travelling fast. Word of mouth and a small window advert are not sufficient to get the crowds you will want to attract, and substantial advertising in the local paper a few days beforehand is essential.

Telephone the author well in advance of the publication date, because if the book is expected to be any good at all, he or she will be in considerable demand already. The celebrity may be in theatre or TV, with a busy schedule that won't allow for last minute requests. Don't be afraid to ask if expenses will be involved – one well known TV personality is reputed to charge £2000 an hour for appearances.

Although the book may be a new title, do make sure that it is actually available, and that you have a good quantity on the day of signing. Quite a few popular books are reprinting by publication day, and unavailable for a short while. You can order a large number on a 'sale or return' basis, so that there is no possibility that you will run out on a successful day.

If there is no fee or only a small amount payable for travel, well and good, but don't forget to provide a few sandwiches and a little wine. Your staff will need to be fully briefed and available throughout the lunch period, which is probably the best time for such sessions. A suitably decked table with the great work in good quantities obviously displayed should be placed centrally in the shop near the window. You should be able to get a showcard from the publisher, and your window-dresser should have been at work a day or so before the event.

Such sessions should not be grand affairs, and you will very often be surprised at how approachable and chatty the celebrity turns out to be. There's no need to rehearse speeches and arrange for bouquets, but a small floral display on the table looks good, and appreciative. If your advertising and general preparation have been effective, you should have a queue forming before the advertised time that the author is due. Equally, you should be prepared for the whole thing to be quite a flop – which may not be your fault, or the author's. For some reason, sometimes, such events simply do not catch on. Bring on the sandwiches and the wine, and make sure of your own signed copy anyway!

If the publisher arranges for an author to visit your shop you will still need to do most of this promotion work. If a promotional tour has been organised to coincide with a new title, you may not be on the planned route. But if you are, you can probably save any travel costs and halve any advertising with the promoting publisher, who will also have arranged for the local rep to be in attendance both beforehand and on the day. Publicity material will be available, and national advertising will have filtered into your area to some degree as well.

Literary luncheons are a variation on the signing session theme, involving a celebrity who is principal guest and speaker at a formal meal. They take quite a lot of organising but they needn't be grand affairs. You can sell tickets from your shop, through the local Information Office or booking agency, and invite a secondary speaker who may be a local celebrity rather than an author. You will have an enjoyable occasion which will get reported in the press, and your guests will be getting more for their money than just the meal.

You will need to organise the arrangements well in advance. Choose a good quality local hotel, who will agree a menu with you for a cost per head and arrange for a suitably sized room to be available, the cost of which should be included in the overall price of the meal. Depending on the importance of the speakers, try to determine the likely maximum number of guests and therefore how many tickets you will sell. The income from ticket sales should at least cover the cost of the meal, any celebrity expenses involved, and any other cost – like printing the tickets – which you may incur.

Tell your local newspaper what you plan to do, and who is coming; invite them along for pre-lunch drinks with the celebrities and suggest they bring along a photographer too. The write-up in that week's local paper is free, and invaluable advertising.

These occasions do not depend on a specific publication day or even a new book, though recent developments, events or new books are bound to be helpful. But again, make sure that there are sufficient quantities of the books you need.

Elaborate multi-course meals should be avoided, and wine should not be included: you will have to choose too cheap a wine for some tastes in order to keep the ticket price reasonable, and some people will prefer not to drink anyway. Take time sorting out the top table, which could include one or two local customers such as the librarian or a company guest. The hotel will give advice on a comfortable layout for the room they have provided, but a top table at right angles to between five and eight tables seating up to ten per table is the likely arrangement.

Indicate to the speakers how long you expect them to be on their feet; about 20 minutes each is the maximum. If your display of their books is discreetly placed near the door, with a member of staff nearby, signed copies can be made available at the end of the formalities.

You should allow yourself a little time before the meal for a quiet drink with the speakers, because here your role is more central than with a shop signing session. You will need to introduce the speakers and say a little about them; even if they are well-known, a small anecdote or little-known point can be made in your very short introduction. Don't spend time extolling the virtues of either the speakers or your shop – both should be evident in the speeches and the success of the occasion, if you have planned it right.

Don't forget to stand up briefly and thank your speakers, your staff and anyone else who has helped in getting the occasion together.

Press reports normally follow unusual or surprising local events and you can't get yourself mentioned just because you speak to a reporter. But if you prepare a short press release every time something worthwhile happens at your shop and send it to the Features Editor (in good time for a photographer to arrive if it is an advance notice), once every so often when things are quiet you may get a mention.

Press releases should be succinctly written, no longer than a page, and double spaced – newspaper editing time is short, so your copy will be corrected if necessary, rather than being retyped.

Receptions in the shop after hours may cost a little bit but here again, if you are promoting a series or particular book, the supplier may halve the cost with you. It's a good idea to have a reception once in a while, simply to say thank you to good customers, and it doesn't cost a fortune. Quite formal invitations should be sent, but you will almost certainly find that 'RSVP' is widely ignored. If you invite 100 people you might expect 15 replies, though of course this depends on whether or not you know the people as regular customers. Even so, some people who said they would come won't turn up, and quite possibly several people you haven't heard from will be first at the door. The invitation should clearly say what time the event starts, and when it ends!

Wine for these receptions should follow the principle of six glasses per bottle, with twice as many bottles of white wine as red. Always take more than you may need on sale or return from the local wine merchant, and don't keep all the bottles on show: there are those who will think the evening doesn't end until the bottles are finished! There should be a light sherry for those who want it, and some fruit juices for non-drinkers.

The invitation should indicate that a light buffet is available. Food for receptions is often over-ordered; for twenty people you could safely have sufficient for fifteen, and don't provide heavy snacks. An evening reception will be either just before or, less likely, just after a meal, and food will be wasted if you are too generous. There is no reason why you should not prepare a light buffet yourself, providing the presentation is good: white tablecloth, flowers and napkins as well as cutlery set off quite humble preparations quite sufficiently.

What do other shops do?

It is essential to look at what other shops do. Not just other bookshops but all your competitors – in other words, just about every other retail outlet in your street and area. Everyone wants to attract the spending customer, who has only so much money. How you persuade him or her to enter your shop rather than the newsagent, wine merchant, Marks and Spencer and so on, is the important point to be made here about marketing and promotion.

Make a point of visiting your neighbourhood shops once in a while, and go in to have a look round. Why do they do what they do? How are their windows laid out? How do their in-store displays work? How obvious are their important products?

Wine merchants are similar to bookshops in terms of customer awareness – see how these shops are presented. Their product is widely varied and variable, with price not always an indicator of quality. Customer awareness of the value of different wines is quite low, and books aren't very different in this respect, since they too are arriving in stock all the time from many different sources, in different guises.

How does your shop compare with others to look at? Is it clean, tidy, *approachable*, does it give *you* confidence? It is difficult to do so, but shop owners should try to see their shops as customers do. Don't forget to ask staff what they think about the things you do and suggest; often they will only express opinions if asked. They'll certainly have ideas too and will be much encouraged if you take some of these ideas up, or ask the staff member to carry out their own plan.

7

Bibliography

Introduction

Booksellers have access to many sources of information about those books that are in print and, to a lesser extent, those out of print. Although the full range of such sources is not always appreciated or for that matter used, it is vital that a bookseller is aware of the sources of information available and how they can be used to provide cost-effective research facilities for the bookshop. It has to be remembered that more than 61 000 new books are published annually in the UK with 560 000 currently in print. You can only represent a small percentage of these in your shop, so the ability to research information about those not stocked becomes an important service, which is an aspect of the bookseller's image and appeal in the market place.

The term 'bibliography' is properly used to cover a wide range of sources of information about books, although in the common parlance of the UK trade, 'bibliography' tends to concentrate on the services provided by J. Whitaker & Sons. In the USA the equivalent service is provided by R. R. Bowker, and a very comprehensive service of the Library of Congress Catalog amongst others. To a lesser extent booksellers also depend on publishers' catalogues although these perhaps do not always attract the attention they deserve. Broadly speaking, the term 'bibliography' is used to cover the history of books, their authorship and editions.

A bibliography can also mean a list of books by a particular author, of a specialist subject or even of a particular publisher or printer; the latter usually applicable to the private presses issuing fine limited editions. By emphasising the range of sources available, it becomes clear that it should be possible to trace details of most books, but whether the time and hence cost involved is justified must be a decision for the individual bookseller.

Booksellers will look to 'the tools of the trade' to give basic information of author, title, publisher, price and possibly ISBN (International Standard Book Number – see p. 115) in a readily accessible and usable form. Most booksellers would expect to find the information needed for a customer in five (possibly ten) minutes at most; thereafter it becomes a job for a more specialist bibliographical source – possibly the local library – as other customers cannot be left unserved for too long. Bibliography could be called 'the great detective story' if all resources are used, and there is great satisfaction in tracing the obscure book, even if no longer available.

Whatever method is used, a bookseller's concern will be that the bibliographies used are a practical aid to finding out quickly about the books that customers need. The key question to be answered when deciding on a particular bibliography will be 'Does it provide a better service to our customers?'. The answer to that, taken objectively, will enable certain bibliographies to be rejected as too specialised for that business, but it will also place on you the responsibility of knowing how to use those that you have selected in an efficient way.

The usual criteria applied to any bibliography are as follows:

a) *Scope*: the limits of the work; the period covered, and frequency of its publications.
b) *Arrangement*: overall presentation of information; is it alpha sequence by author or by title? Separately or are they mixed?
c) *Bibliographical details*: what information is given, and hence how can it be used?
d) *Special features*: what additional information is included e.g. publishers' addresses; ISBNs; special bibliography; description of book's contents or background to individual authors.

These criteria should be applied equally to a major tool of the trade or to a small personal catalogue. No one bibliographic system will necessarily give the answer to all enquiries, so a search of a number may be necessary. 'Trade' bibliographies are produced to reduce the searching to a minimum, and deal with the sort of questions regularly asked by the customer, and hence the bookseller.

The usual questions to which you will need answers are:

1 What titles are available and, by inference, which are out of print?
2 What other books has a particular author written?
3 Where the author and/or title is known, who is the publisher?
4 What is the latest price? In what editions is the book available?
5 What titles have been available in the past by a particular author but are no longer in print?
6 What books are there available on a particular, often highly specialised, subject?

Whitaker's sources

J. Whitaker & Sons Ltd (Whitaker's) offer a comprehensive range of bibliographical sources which are widely used both in the UK and internationally. To keep the service up to date, they are dependent on publishers providing the necessary bibliographical details by completing a pro forma (the yellow form). Inevitably some titles are not listed immediately because a publisher fails to send the information, either through oversight or through ignorance of the system. However, Whitaker's search other bibliographies, such as the British National Bibliography (BNB, see p. 117), to ensure that their information is as complete as possible.

Despite any such minor limitations the service provided, if understood and used effectively, will answer most of the bookseller's bibliographical queries accurately. Therefore Whitaker's in one form or another is a 'must' for any bookshop. Selecting the most useful service is up to the individual bookshop, depending particularly on its policy towards customers' special orders, as well as the financial implications of the decision to subscribe to one part of the service rather than another. All services described are also available on magnetic tape for computer users.

Whitaker's Books in Print (Microfiche)

Previously known as *British Books in Print* and hence referred to as BBIP, this monthly service provides the booksellers with approximately 80 microfiche, listing in excess of 450 000 titles in print and over 3000 titles due for publication in the following two months. 5000 new titles are added and 3000 out of print titles removed monthly. The service also includes a listing of over 12 000 publishers with their address and telephone number in alphabetical and ISBN prefix sequence.

A microfiche (measuring 15 cm × 10.5 cm) is made of transparent durable plastic and contains 269 single column pages at a reduction of 48×. Each fiche is clearly titled at the top giving details of the alphabetical range and the date with sequential numbering to facilitate filing. A durable binder is supplied with the initial order. It is of course necessary to purchase a microfiche reader before the system can be used. The cost of the reader and the annual subscription is approximately four times that of the bound edition (see below), but it is generally agreed that this is an extremely cost-effective means of providing information quickly to the customer, and probably deals with 90% of enquiries at a first search.

The Entry of Bibliographical Details

Each entry gives author (known as the main entry and printed in bold type); editor where appropriate; size of book; the number of pages including preliminaries if appropriate; whether illustrated or not and, if so, the number of illustrations; editions (paperbacks are marked pbk; if this is not indicated then it is deemed to be hardback); price – this is a net price unless an asterisk* is included which means non-net; publisher; month and year of publication; and ISBN (International Standard Book Number).

Whitaker's Books in Print (Bound edition)

Previously known as *British Books in Print* (BBIP) and published annually in November in four volumes which contain all books in print at the end of March in the year of publication. The arrangement is alpha sequence by author, title or subject if the subject word forms a key part of the title, particularly applicable to annual reference publications. The range of titles is similar to that described for the microfiche edition. The prelims include guidance on how to use this source of information, a glossary of abbreviations used, a numerical listing of ISBNs of publishers, and a bibliography of books about the book trade as well as a list of series with their publishers.

Whitaker's Bookbank CD-ROM Service

CD-ROM stands for Compact Disc – Read Only Memory. This is physically identical to an audio disc, being 4¾″ in diameter, and contains 30 miles of book listing. It is issued monthly and provides all the information available in *Whitaker's Books in Print* for use with an IBMPC or truly compatible computer. It provides various modes of access and methods of displaying information, as well as interfacing with Teleordering (see p. 24). This service was launched in January 1988 and presents an exciting breakthrough for booksellers in the obtaining of information more quickly and comprehensively than is possible using the microfiche service.

The Bookseller* including *Publications of the Week

This is published weekly on Friday by Whitakers and is the main journal for the whole book trade. It contains news, views, reports and articles on relevant aspects of the trade, as well as advertising from publishers announcing forthcoming books on special promotion, and is therefore required reading for any bookseller. From the bibliographical point of view, *The Bookseller* includes a vital section 'Publications of the Week' which lists current titles in classified sections alphabetically by author, and forms the basis of the information presented in the other Whitaker bibliographies.

Many bibliographers would maintain that all research should start from the latest date of information and then you should work backwards; in practice most booksellers turn to *Whitaker's Books in Print* and then, if necessary, investigate other sources.

***The Bookseller* – Spring and Autumn issues**

Twice a year in February and August these special editions of *The Bookseller* are published. Historically, these were known as the Export numbers because they were aimed particularly at the overseas market to announce forthcoming publications. The value of these issues is that each deals with titles due for publication in the next six months. The first few pages draw attention to important titles under the heading 'Highlights of the Season'. Thereafter, over 200 pages are devoted to a survey of books to be published under various classifications.

The remaining 500 or more pages are devoted to publishers' advertisements, these being effectively publishers' catalogues in support of the books mentioned in the survey. The remaining pages are an alpha sequence section giving author, titles, price, publisher and ISBN, only without the usual detailed information associated with the Whitaker services. An index to advertisers completes the volume. The scope of these issues could be said to be limited because only those books advertised are in the index. However, most important publishers do support these issues, and the editorial comment is invaluable for planning forward buying. Special microfiches of the 'Index to Books Advertised' are available.

Whitaker's Books of the Month and Books to Come

This includes an alpha sequence of author and title for all books published in the calendar month, based on the previous four or five weekly issues of *Publications of the Week* in *The Bookseller*. Also included are details of books due to be published in the next two months; these are clearly marked with a star in the left-hand margin before the entry. A commentary on forthcoming books is given and a report on publishers' errors in the wrong allocation of ISBNs. Because similar information is provided in *Whitaker's Books in Print* on microfiche, this source is not as widely used as it could be. There are obviously practical advantages in using a printed source of information to check stock profiles, or that books subscribed have been received, rather than wading through microfiche entries.

Whitaker's Book List

Previously known as *Whitaker's Cumulative Book List* (CBL), this is published annually in hardback. By carefully accumulating the weekly issues of the *Publications of the Week* in *The Bookseller*, which are replaced by the monthly *Whitaker's Books of the Month and Books to Come*, the bookseller will always have up-to-date information available. The twelve monthly issues of *Whitaker's Books of the Month and Books to Come* are cumulated into *Whitaker's Book List*, published in hardback. This gives a permanent record of books published in a particular year; it is not affected by the fact that books go out of print and are therefore 'lost' from *Whitaker's Books in Print* services.

Whitaker's Classified Monthly Book List

This monthly publication lists books under author with the usual detailed information, but arranged within the 138 classifications used by Whitaker's which have been derived from the Dewey Decimal Classification and UNESCO (see below). The accuracy of the classification is dependent on the quality of the publishers' information. The list covers those books published in the particular month plus forthcoming books for two months ahead if the information has been supplied by the relevant publisher.

The 138 classifications used by Whitakers are as follows:

Agriculture
Air Transport
Aircraft (Civil)
Aircraft (Military)
Anthropology
Antique Furniture
Archaeology
Architecture & Town Planning
Art, General
Art (Ceramics)
Art (Drawing and Painting)
Art (Sculpture)
Astronomy
Atlases & Maps
Bibliographies
Biography
Biology
Botany
Building
Careers
Chemistry
Children's Books
Cinema & Television
Communication Services
Computer Games
Computers, General
Computers (Hardware)
Computers (Software)
Costume
Criminology
Customs & Folklore
Dentistry
Economics
Education
Engineering, General
Engineering (Civil)
Engineering (Electrical)
Engineering (Electronic)
Entertainment
Fiction, General
Food & Drink
Forestry
Gardening
Genealogy
General Knowledge
Geography
Geology & Palaeontology
Handicrafts & Printmaking
Health & Hygiene
History, General
History (First World War)
History (Second World War)
History (Africa)
History (Ancient)
History (Asia)
History (Australasia)
History (Europe)
History (Great Britain)
History (North America)
History (South & Central America)
Household Management
Humour
Indoor Games
Industrial Chemistry
Language
Law
Library Science & Publishing
Literature
Management & Business Administration
Mathematics
Medicine
Meteorology
Military Science
Music
Numismatics
Nursing
Occult
Psychology
Public Administration
Railways
Religion
Road Transport
Road Vehicles (Civil)
Road Vehicles (Military)
School Textbooks
Science, General
Shipping & Inland Waterways
Ships (Civil)
Ships (Military)
Social Sciences
Social Welfare
Soil & Crop Science
Sport, General
Sport (Athletics)
Sport (Combat Sports)
Sport (Cricket)
Sport (Motor Sports)
Sport (Riding)
Sport (Rugby)
Sport (Soccer)
Sport (Tennis)
Stamps & Stamp Collecting
Stockbreeding & Veterinary Science
Technology & Manufacturing
Theatre
Trade & Commerce
Transport, General
Travel, General
Travel Accommodation
Travel (Africa)
Travel (Asia)
Travel (Australasia)
Travel (Europe)
Travel (Great Britain)
Travel (North America)

Fiction, Historical
Fiction, Mystery
Fiction, Romance
Fiction, Science Fiction
Fiction, Short Stories
Fiction, War
Fiction, Westerns
Fishing & Hunting
Pets
Philosophy
Photography
Physics
Plays
Poetry
Political Science
Psychiatry
Travel (South & Central America)
Zoology, General
Zoology (Birds)
Zoology (Fishes)
Zoology (Insects)
Zoology (Mammals)
Zoology (Reptiles & Amphibians)

Books 1976–89 Now OP (microfiche)

This records on more than 30 microfiche over 220 000 titles published between 1976 and 1989 which were out of print at the end of May 1989. Included are fiche which give the names and addresses of publishers whose titles are listed and who are still in business. ISBNs in numerical sequence are also included. This is updated annually; the starting year (1976) remains unchanged but obviously ‘ – 89’ will change in successive years, as will the number of fiche and entries.

Bookbank OP

This is the CD-ROM service covering the same information as the microfiche, published annually.

Religious Books in Print

This lists over 24 000 titles in print with their publishers plus a classified index which used 18 principal classifications (e.g. ‘G’ = Doctrine: Subjects (Christian), which is then subdivided into 127 subsidiary subjects, e.g. G1 = Creation and Trinity, or G4 = Church). Also included is a directory of 1400 publishers and distributors.

Children’s Books in Print

Another special annual Whitaker catalogue listing over 29 000 titles in print from over 1000 publishers, and including a classified index of 98 subject categories (e.g. C1 = Non-fiction – Africa; Yesterday and Today, or C90 = Football).

ISBNs – What are they?

Reference has been made to the ISBN (International Standard Book Number) and to SBN (Standard Book Number) in the description of the Whitaker’s service. It seems appropriate at this point to outline the scheme which plays a vital part in bibliography, especially where computers, EPOS (Electronic Point of Sale) cash registers or Teleordering are involved.

The basic idea is that each title published should have a unique and simple identifying number. A book numbering scheme was introduced into the UK in 1967. The ISBN scheme was developed internationally from that, following a meeting in London in 1968 attended by representatives from Britain, America, Eire, the Netherlands, Denmark, France, West Germany and Norway, with an observer from UNESCO.

Each ISBN consists of ten digits which are divided into four parts of variable length separated by a space or a hyphen; in practice, of course, a computer can deal with the numbers without spacing. The first part – the Group identifier – identifies national or geographic groupings of publication; for example, 0 or 1 comes from main English-speaking countries such as the UK, USA, Eire, Canada, New Zealand, Australia and South Africa; the prefix for France is 2; Germany 3 and the Netherlands 90.

The second part – the publisher identifier – indicates a particular publisher. Publishers with large outputs are allocated short prefixes, and those with small outputs have longer prefixes. For example, Collins are allocated 00 and Collier Macmillan 02, ABP use 415 and the BBC 563; but the Booksellers Association has 907972, and Ansells (the Brewers) uses a seven digit number 9507009.

The third part is used for a particular title or edition of a title allocated by the publisher, and the fourth and final section at the end of the ISBN provides an automatic check on the correctness of the ISBN. This is a computer check digit which is calculated electronically to detect incorrectly transcribed numbers, although this can also be calculated manually rather laboriously. To quote from the *ISBN User's Manual* 'the check digit is calculated on a modulus 11 with weights 10–2, using X in lieu of 10 where ten would occur as a check digit'.

For example:

0	340	42876	7
↑	↑	↑	↑
International Prefix/UK	*Publisher*	*Title/Editor*	*Computer Check Digit*

The scheme is administered internationally by the International Standard Book Number Agency in Berlin, with group agencies in various countries; for example 0 and 1 have separate agencies in the USA, Britain, Canada, etc. with the main agency for the whole group in the UK, based at Whitaker's.

The ISBN may appear printed as such and/or as a bar code for light wand or laser beam 'reading'.

Every 6 months, Whitaker's issue *International Standard Book Numbers Listing* on microfiche which includes over 900 000 titles from their masterfile, including nearly 50% of out of print books, in ISBN sequence.

ISSN

A complementary numbering system for serial publications including periodicals, year books and monographic series has also been set up, known as the International Standard Serial Number scheme, administered by the International Serial Data System in Paris. A British office is attached to the British Library in London.

Some publications may in certain circumstances bear an ISBN and an ISSN but where both are assigned, both must be clearly identified.

British National Bibliography (BNB)

You should be aware of this system, as it is widely used by librarians, and specialist and university booksellers, though seldom found in 'general' bookshops.

BNB has been produced since 1950 by librarians working for the British Library Bibliographic Services Division. Its objectives are to catalogue every new book published in the British Isles and to give the subject matter of each book as precisely as possible.

The books, which are catalogued by means of the Dewey Decimal Classifications system, are those received under the Copyright Acts 1911 and 1963, as amended by the British Library Act 1972. These Acts require publishers to supply one copy of each of their publications to the Copyright Receipt Office of the Library within one month of publication.

In practice, the idea of a national listing of all books published in the UK (with a British or Republic of Ireland imprint) is nearly achieved. However some small publishers are ignorant of the Act, or may deliberately ignore it, as they do not want to give copies away especially if a highly priced limited edition is involved.

BNB is published weekly with monthly cumulations, followed by four-monthly cumulations covering the periods January to April and from May to August. These are finally published in two hardback volumes covering the whole year. Cumulations exist for earlier years with the initial volumes covering periods of four years. But as publishing output increased this became an annual volume, and now two such volumes are necessary for each year.

Central to BNB is the use of the Dewey Decimal Classification system, devised by the American Melvil Dewey in 1837. This Classification system is widely used in the British public library system. Basically, there are ten main classifications which can be divided into 999 subject classifications; beyond that, there follows the decimal point from which the numbering could carry on in theory to infinity. The main classifications are:

0 general
100 philosophy
200 religion
300 social sciences
400 linguistics
500 pure science
600 applied science and technology
700 fine arts and recreation
800 literature
900 history, including geography and biography

The subject classifications have a 'form' so that

503 is a dictionary of pure science
603 is a dictionary of applied science
703 is a dictionary of art
803 is a dictionary of world literature.

In practical terms BNB can locate books by subject, which would not be possible through Whitaker. If a customer asked for a book on Mary Queen of Scots, it would only be possible to trace it using Whitaker's bibliographies if the words 'Mary' or 'Scots' were mentioned in the title. But supposing the book had a hypothetical title like 'James' Daughter'. Using BNB, it would be possible to locate this by use of the Dewey Decimal Classification because:

941 is the History of the British Isles
941.1 is the History of Scotland
941.105 covers the Reformation 1542–1603, which includes the period of Mary Queen of Scots.

You would then refer to 941.105 until you had traced the book in one of the issues of BNB.

CIP Data

CIP stands for Cataloging in Publication. A publisher submits the prelims or the page proofs of a forthcoming title and a catalogue slip. The entry is prepared within 10 days and is printed in the weekly BNB entry marked 'CIP entry' giving price fixed at that time (generally at least eight weeks before the expected publication date). The CIP entry is amended when titles are published and deposited at the Copyright Receipt Office; the weekly list then identifies the book as 'CIP rev'.

CIP information is supplied back to the publisher and can be printed on the back (verso) of the title page as a catalogue entry for the book, libraries who have bought it can add the details to the library catalogue.

An example of CIP
Loizos, Peter
The heart grown bitter.
1. Cyprus—Politics and government
2. Cyprus—History
1. Title
956.45′04 D554.9

ISBN 0–521–24230–4
ISBN 0–521–28546–1 Pbk

Books in English (BIE)

A major microfiche bibliography of English language titles published throughout the world. In excess of 100 000 titles are recorded annually. It is produced from the records of the British Library Bibliographic Services and the United States Library of

Congress. All subjects are covered including fiction. Two-monthly snowballing cumulations culminate in an annual listing. The 1971–80 cumulation contains 1.1 million entries on 600 fiche in a compact case. Annual listings for 1981–5 are available.

BLAISE-LINE

The British Library offer a computer service known as BLAISE-LINE (*B*ritish *L*ibrary *A*utomated *I*nformation *SE*rvice) which makes available over 2 million bibliographic records, kept up to date by the use of MARC (*MA*chine *R*eadable *C*atalogue) topics with a control computer located at Harlow.

This includes the BNB database back to 1950 (when BNB was started), the Whitaker's database plus all Library of Congress (USA) records, irrespective of language or country of origin, since 1968. Additionally, another database records a range of audio-visual material and also the Conference Proceedings Index and the British Education Index. Further additions are planned.

Book Data

A relative newcomer to the scene is Book Data. This is a marketing-orientated bibliographic service which is subscription-based, with publishers paying to have details of their titles listed.

Book Data differs from other databases because, in the interests of accuracy, information is actively collected from various departments within the publishing houses. Book Data also undertakes to complete the CIP (see p. 119) details for publishers, thus ensuring information about new books is logged quickly with the British Library's British National Bibliography.

Book Data's title records contain a wide range of bibliographic data elements: not only are the usual details of author, title, price, publisher, etc. included, but also the academic and professional affiliations of the authors or editors, a short description of the book, and a full contents list (where appropriate). Book Data have their own system of subject classification, with over 1300 categories, and all books are given a readership level (e.g. undergraduate, teenage, research, etc.). Dewey and the American Library of Congress numbers are given where known. Finally, and possibly most importantly, all these data elements are indexed and are fully searchable: searches can be combined, meaning that a user could, for example, ask for a list of new books by Harvard professors, priced at between £10 and £50, to be published in March on the subject of gastro-enterology, with a postgraduate readership level.

Subscribers can choose the way in which they take information from the database. Usually a customer profile is established for a potential subscriber, who selects the subject areas and readership levels in which he is interested, and which parts of the record he requires (he may, for example, not need the full contents list, or may only want specific bibliographic details). Each month he will receive information about the new titles within his chosen area. He can also choose how far in advance of publication he wants to be advised of details. Subscribers may also take information on an *ad hoc* basis, calling for listings or factsheets as and when they need them.

The information can be relayed to the user in a variety of forms: on magnetic tape or floppy disk for those who want to load the data straight into their computer system, or on paper for those who are not computerised. The complete database on CD-ROM, and a more selective PC-based system (which comes complete with its own search software and monthly-updated data files) are also available.

The main use of such systems can be either as a source of high quality new title records ready for loading onto the bookseller's own database (thus saving time and money), or for creating detailed subject listings for promotional and marketing purposes (the information can be fed into the bookseller's word-processing or desktop publishing system and redesigned into a catalogue with a personalised order-form, for example).

One drawback to the Book Data database so far is that, because publishers have to pay to have titles included, the database is not yet complete, but it is expanding daily. At the time of writing, Book Data estimates that there are around 250 000 titles on the system, which is expected to rise to 300 000 by the end of 1990.

USA Bibliographies

R. R. Bowker's services

Bowker's are the American equivalent of Whitaker's; their bibliographies have much in common, with *Books in Print USA* paralleling *Whitaker's Books in Print*. Annual hardback editions are available in seven volumes, three covering authors, three covering titles and the final one listing publishers and their addresses and other information. The service is available on microfiche, and on CD-ROM known as *Books in Print Plus*. Also available are *Subject Guide to Books in Print*, with regular supplements; *Forthcoming Books* and *Subject Guide to Forthcoming Books*, with a number of specialist *Books in Print*. *Paperback Books in Print* is published in the spring and autumn, and is the one most usually found in UK bookshops, who generally do not subscribe to Bowker's services.

The Library of Congress Catalog

Although unlikely to be used by booksellers, this is to be found in some university libraries. The following outlines the system used, as the Library of Congress basic classification is shown on the British Library Cataloguing in Publication (CIP) entry found on the verso of the title page of books (see p. 119).

The Library of Congress was founded in 1800 by the Congress of the United States. Its first source of material is the Copyright Office of the United States. Approximately one third is books, a second third is composed of periodicals including both popular magazines and learned journals, and the final third consists of tens of thousands of sheets of music. Additionally, there is a miscellany of maps, telephone directories, photographs, cannisters containing motion pictures and some computer tapes. All of this arises from the American method of protecting ownership of creative works. Documents of the Federal Government and of State Governments in the USA are included. There is a complex international network for the purchase and exchange of books worldwide, as well as gift arrangements.

Such a vast international collection not only requires effective organisation procedures but also a precise classification system called the Library of Congress Catalog, to which reference has been made earlier. Each book or piece of material has to be catalogued into one subject only and be converted into a numerical code. New codes are being devised within the system each year to reflect the expansion of man's experience. The *Library of Congress Subject Heading List* exceeds 1500 pages to cope with the large range of subjects; additionally and equally important is the *Library of Congress Classification Schedules* which contain the 'call' numbers which go on the spines of the books to bring like subjects together. The Library of Congress classifications system is based on letters and numbers and can in theory offer 676 subject divisions.

Main classes are marked with a single letter; for example, J covers political science and K covers Law. By doubling letters and adding numbers, the system becomes very detailed so JA covers collections and general works of political science and JC political theory. There is no natural progression within this system. HF is Commerce and one might expect, following the logic of Dewey, that 'Finance' would be a sub-division of this; in fact, Finance has its own classification – HG. 'Public Finance' is deemed to be a classification separate from 'Finance' and accordingly is designated HJ.

By the addition of numbers, further accurate classifications are possible. The result is thousands of specifically allocated numbers for thousands of topics, organised precisely but not necessarily in a logical progression, so that the system cannot be learned and so it is essential to look it up. The range of classification can be extended to two letters, four numerals, one decimal number, a decimal letter and a number combination to locate a particular title on the shelf.

The catalogued information is marketed on cards to libraries and is available as already mentioned to UK booksellers and librarians on the computer base of BLAISE-LINE.

Publishers' catalogues

The bookseller should not forget the value of an individual publisher's catalogue. The publisher invests money and time in the production of these, and the bibliographical information can be fuller than that found in any of the sources already dealt with. Too many publishers' catalogues are just filed or thrown away without proper study. The amount of useful information varies depending on the purpose for which the catalogue is produced. Some can be used for marketing books to customers, whereas others are mainly useful for reference. A useful tip is always to put the date received on the cover, so that at a later date its currency can be assessed. Publisher's catalogues can be classified into five main categories:–

1 The General or Complete Catalogue is usually issued annually and lists all books in print at the time of preparation of the catalogue; that is likely to be two to three months before actual issue of the catalogue. A good catalogue will state the date at which it is compiled. You would expect to find in such catalogues the author/editor, title, edition, price, year of publication and ISBN. Forthcoming titles are not usually included.

2 Seasonal lists are issued as necessary according to the size of the publisher; usually in the spring and autumn and frequently for the summer and winter, to announce forthcoming books. These usually contain full details of the book, often accompanied by a photograph of the author or an illustration of the cover, but price and publication date may be only provisional.

3 Subject lists tend to come from school book publishers and higher education publishers. Any publisher may, however, issue such a list if they have a particularly strong classification, for example History or Economics, Law or Medicine.

4 Educational lists are similar to subject lists but cover the publisher's complete academic range. These are frequently mailed direct to school and colleges, or are used by the school or academic rep, rather than by the bookseller. You would expect such lists to cover those titles predominantly supplied in bulk, i.e. textbooks which are usually non-net.

5 Stock lists are sent to booksellers for information by paperback publishers. These are primarily designed for the rep, or for use by the bookseller as an order form, and are usually arranged as a 'picking list' for the publisher's warehouse staff. Such lists have limited use in bibliographical terms, except to check whether a title is available.

Format of Catalogues

The lack of uniformity of size often presents the bookseller with storage problems, but a catalogue should not be discarded because it is an awkward size if it has bibliographical value.

Many bookshops file catalogues in a filing cabinet; others prefer to use stout cardboard folders. It is essential to replace old catalogues with new, but ensure that information about any book delayed in publication is extracted from the previous catalogue if it is not in the latest one. This emphasises the need to examine each one closely.

Factors to Check With Any Catalogue

a) Does it list authors in alphabetical sequence?
b) Are authors and titles in one complete alphabet, or are author and title listings separate?
c) Is it arranged by Dewey Decimal Classification, as found with the Oxford University Press General Catalogue?
d) How are subjects and series dealt with?
e) Are out of print titles included, or indicated in any way?
f) Is the index accurate and helpful?
g) How do publishing groups deal with their subsidiary companies?
   Do you know which companies belong to which groups?
   How will you file these?
h) Are classifications listed under headings you might not have considered? For example, fiction can be classified separately under such headings as 'romantic' or 'bestsellers' or 'detective', or the fiction listing may be all mixed up.

Other Sources

One important source of information is the general reference books to be found on the bookshelves. Some of these may usefully be added to the bibliographical reference section of the bookshop, depending on the market being served.

Chambers Biographical Dictionary and the *Dictionary of National Biography* (Oxford University Press) both give details of authors' lives and works; the former internationally and the latter nationally. *Who's Who* (A&C Black, published annually) and *Who was Who* both include titles and year of publication (but not publisher) of books written by people listed in those reference books. For more out of the way enquiries, the *Oxford Companion to English Literature* is useful; the same applies to the other Oxford Companions.

When evaluating any book, note should be taken of the further reading lists and bibliographical references to source material that may be given at the end of the book or at the end of each chapter. Look for lists of other works by that author or other books in the same series, or from that particular publisher on related subjects.

Information about books can be gleaned by being generally aware, by listening to radio and watching television programmes, or reading newspapers. Books are only mentioned or reviewed if they are newsworthy and for no other reason. A review page in a newspaper (for example the *Sunday Times* or the *Guardian*) is there to help sell the newspaper; but the benefits that accrue to the book trade are an invaluable spin-off in terms of free advertising. Weeklies such as the *Times Literary Supplement, The Listener*, the *Times Higher Education Supplement*, or *The Economist* may be necessary reading for many general booksellers, as *History Today*, the *Railway Magazine* or *Stamp Monthly* may be to specialists. It is not sufficient just to be aware of this sort of information; it should be used to help you increase your sales of books.

Tie-ins with films, looking at other bookshops, contact with local specialist societies, information from Book Trust or the Booksellers Associations' Marketing Initiative are all sources of information which may suggest new marketing opportunities. This type of information may need selective treatment by the bookseller, who would be well advised to set up some sort of card index, possibly within the stock control systems. Information stored but not employed is useless; it must be available for positive action to increase sales in the short term or long term if the time devoted to recording it is to be justified.

Knowing how to use the various tools of the trade should not just be seen as an academic exercise, but as an effective and positive way to create additional sales in previously untried markets, as well as providing a high degree of customer service.

8

Introducing Technology

Advances in technology over the past few years have brought computerisation within the reach of all but the smallest bookseller. There is now a vast array of systems available which claim to do almost everything for you except put the book in the customer's bag! The trade is finally switching on and many of the pundits have said that those who fail to keep abreast of developments and make optimum use of them will fall by the wayside in what is forecast as being the retailing boom of the 1990s.

Basically, computerisation of the book trade falls roughly into three areas:

1 Computerisation of bookshop systems
2 Electronic book trade communications networks
3 Information technology (e.g. bibliographic databases).

Let's look at the first area, which will be of most interest and relevance to you.

Bookshop Systems

In all likelihood, the small bookshop's use of technology will be centred on a personal computer, comprising a VDU (or screen), a keyboard and a printer. Depending on the software used, this system will be able to cope with everything from basic accounting procedures and payroll through to sophisticated stock control (although for this you will need extra equipment at point-of-sale, such as barcode readers and compatible cash registers).

What your system will do for you and your business will ultimately depend on

a) how much you are prepared to spend and
b) how much research, time and care you are prepared to give at the setting-up stage.

Most of the horror stories you will undoubtedly hear on this subject are the result of skimping on the second point.

The uses of some of the above-mentioned computerised procedures, such as accounting and stock control, are covered in more detail in earlier chapters.

Electronic Communications Networks

To a certain extent, electronic communication within the book trade is still in its infancy. The full potential of all the component parts of the trade (retailer, supplier, library, information provider) being able to talk to each other and send vital information quickly and accurately has not yet been realised.

In many ways the book trade is lucky in that it lends itself to technology in having such an advanced product coding system – the ISBN. This identifier (and all the bibliographic information it represents), both in its original format and as an EAN (European Article Number) barcode, can be transmitted in many ways already: what is currently being worked on by many book trade parties is the problem of communications standards. Although the trade as a whole works well together, its existing methods of communications are somewhat fragmented and need regulating. However, there is one communications system which will probably be of great use to you – Teleordering.

Teleordering is covered in detail on pp. 24–27, and if the words 'electronic communications network' sound daunting to you, remember that this is exactly what Teleordering is: it is a way for booksellers to communicate their book orders electronically via a central computerised clearing house to their suppliers (i.e. publishers and wholesalers). The system has been in operation since 1978, and is currently installed in over 1000 retail sites in the UK. One day soon, Teleordering, or a system such as this, will be responsible for sending other information between publisher and bookseller: invoices, queries on availability and payments will all be passed between companies at the press of a button, making everyday procedures streamlined and more accurate.

Information Technology

Until 1978 the bookseller's main bibliographic reference tool, *Whitaker's Books in Print* (at that time known as *British Books in Print*), was available only in printed volumes. Then came the first technological revolution in the form of information presented on microfiche. Until recently, then, this information has been available only in printed or microfiche form, although other more specialised areas, such as the library community, have had more advanced systems for some time.

However, in the past two or three years there has been much pioneering work done in the area of computerisation of bibliographic databases, and one solution has been found in compact disc technology. 1988 saw the launch of the *Whitaker's Books in Print* database as *Whitaker's Bookbank CD-ROM*, providing the whole of *Books in Print* on one compact disc updated monthly. For the bookseller, the revolution does not lie simply in the physical presentation of the database, but in the active way in which he can search the information, produce lists from it via a printer, and use it to create stockfiles for his own computer system. (*Bookbank* is covered further on p. 115.)

There are other computerised databases (some of which are described in this book), each one of particular interest to different users in the book trade. Advances in the provision of bibliographical information can help you as a bookseller to offer a more sophisticated service to your customers and thus generate more business.

The Future

Technology is progressing at such a speed that it is impossible to predict how it will feature in bookshops in even twenty years' time. Already it is possible to look for a title, locate it, categorise it, transfer its full details to a bookshop stock control programme, and place an order for it at the press of a few buttons. Technology is already being applied to distribution at the supplier's end of the operation, which means that deliveries are becoming quicker.

All that can be predicted is that anyone who wants to make a go of bookselling, stay in business and make a profit cannot afford to ignore advances in technology. The BA has produced a simple guide to all these areas plus advice on setting up a bookshop computer system (including lists of suppliers, etc.). The *BA Bookshop Computer Guide* is available from the Booksellers Association.

9

Law for Booksellers

Anyone involved in running any kind of business needs to be aware of legislation which may affect their trading – this is likely to include company law, employment law, law relating to premises, etc. For a retailer, understanding consumer law is essential. We shall look briefly at this general legislation later on.

However, for booksellers there are several other pieces of legislation which relate specifically to the book trade, and which it is vital that you fully understand. These are:

1 The Net Book Agreement
2 Copyright Law
3 Legislation on Libel and Obscenity

The Net Book Agreement

This is the most important legal consideration governing retail bookselling, and is a form of regulation most commonly referred to as resale price maintenance (r.p.m.) At present, r.p.m. applies only to two commodities in the UK, brand-name pharmaceuticals and books, and it is this which regulates the prices at which these goods may be sold to the public.

The NBA came into being on 1st January 1900 and r.p.m. for books has twice since been upheld in the courts, with rulings that it is not against the public interest. Briefly, the NBA is the means by which publishers fix the price of their books, below which they may not be sold to the public or end consumer. Every publisher is at liberty to decide whether or not he declares a title to be 'net', that is, price-fixed, or non-net. A non-net title carries a recommended or list price, but its price is not fixed and the bookseller may sell at a discount. The NBA does not set a maximum price limit – a net book may be sold at more than the fixed net price but not below, except under certain circumstances (see p. 135).

So, what is the difference between net and non-net books, and how can the bookseller differentiate between the two?

Net books are usually those which you would expect to find on the shelves of a general, High Street bookshop, i.e. popular, general interest, everyday books. You can usually tell a net book by the fact that its price will be printed on its cover, or on the inside of the jacket. It may read £4.50 net(t), or simply £4.50; the addition of the word net(t) is not important.

Non-net books are nearly always school textbooks or educational titles and, often, religious books and many editions of the Bible.

The basic reasoning behind deciding which books should be net or non-net is as follows. The publisher assumes that when a bookseller places an order for educational school books, it will be on behalf of a school or institutional customer who is likely to have made a firm order for multiple copies. The bookseller is therefore involved in a fairly low-risk transaction, and the publisher accordingly supplies the books at a lower discount (usually 17½%, or approximately half the average net book trade discount of 35%). As we have said, the prices of these non-net books are not fixed, thereby allowing the bookseller to negotiate the terms of supply with his institutional customer. Many local authorities invite tenders for non-net book supply at the beginning of each financial year, and this is one of the few times when booksellers may compete with one another on a price basis.

If supplying non-net books to institutions in response to firm orders is a relatively low-risk transaction, then buying stock and new titles to sell in a shop is virtually the opposite. Apart from relying on his buying skills, the bookseller has no way of guaranteeing when he will see a financial return on the capital outlayed to purchase his stock – a book which may take three months to sell will probably have been paid for within thirty days. For taking this risk, the publisher allows the bookseller a higher trade discount on net books than for non-net, usually 35%.

Apart from the difference in discount (which may not always be applied), booksellers can identify non-net books in the following ways:

a) by the asterisk* appearing after the price on *Whitaker's Books in Print*
b) from publishers' catalogues
c) most accurately, from the publisher's invoice accompanying the goods.

Why Have A Net Book Agreement?
The Net Book Agreement was instituted at the turn of the century, following pressure from booksellers on publishers to stem the tide of discounting that was threatening to put an end to the existence of stockholding bookshops selling 'good' books. At that time, many booksellers were forced to sell a range of other goods in order to make a living and as a result were stocking only the bestsellers of the day. In 1890, Macmillan took action and published the first 'net' book, and ten years later the NBA officially came into being. Recently, however, there has been an increase in opposition to the NBA and discounting has started to occur.

In spite of changes in the trade and the economic climate, the arguments then in favour of a fixed price for some books still hold true today. At the hearing of the NBA case in the Restrictive Practices Court, the 1962 judgement stated that

'. . . abrogation of the Net Book Agreement would produce the following results: the number of stockholding booksellers in the country would be reduced. The stocks held by the surviving stockholding booksellers would be less extensive and less varied than at present. Although in rare cases retail purchasers might be able to buy particular titles more cheaply than if the Agreement remained in force, the retail price of most books would be higher. Fewer titles would be published, and those which failed to find a publisher in consequence of the altered conditions resulting from the abrogation of the Agreement would probably include works of literary or scholastic value. In each of these respects we think that individual members of the book-buying public would be denied benefits or advantages which they would enjoy, or be likely to enjoy, as purchasers and users of books if the Agreement were to continue in force. Booksellers of all kinds as purchasers of books would be adversely affected by the increase in prices of books, for, as we have pointed out, this increase would exceed any increase which might occur in booksellers' discounts. Booksellers as purchasers would also be adversely affected by the decrease in the number of titles published, resulting in a less wide and varied field of choice. The decrease would similarly adversely affect the reading public in general as users of books whether bought or borrowed, and borrowers from public or commercial libraries as users of books would be adversely affected to the extent that by reason of higher prices the libraries would be compelled to hold more restricted stocks.

These consequences can be summarised as (1) fewer and less well-equipped stockholding bookshops, (2) more expensive books, (3) fewer published titles.'

The Enforcement of the NBA

The NBA is passed to retailers as a Condition of Sale. The Publishers Association upholds the Net Book Agreement, which requires that publishers ensure that their net books are not sold at below the net price, except within the terms of the NBA. A publisher may still publish net books if he does not belong to the PA, and even if he is not a signatory to the Agreement. (Signatories and PA members are, of course, still at liberty to publish non-net titles.) The NBA was registered with the Registrar of Restrictive Trading Agreements, following the implementation of the Restrictive Trade Practice Act of 1956, which outlawed collective price maintenance, unless it could be justified as not being against the public interest.

In 1968, books were exempted from the provisions of the Resale Price Act 1964, thereby giving publishers the authority to fix their prices and to ensure that their net prices were observed.

As we have said, the NBA is passed from the publisher to the retailer as a Condition of Sale, the terms of which generally appear on the publisher's invoice. The act of accepting goods is a tacit agreement by the retailer that the Standard Conditions of Sale will be observed. Failure to do so can ultimately lead to legal action, with the publisher seeking a Court injunction to prevent the offending bookseller from selling his goods in breach of the NBA. Both the Publishers and Booksellers Associations are active in investigating and discouraging infringements of the Agreement, although it is the PA who are ultimately empowered to take action in infringements on behalf of their members.

It is worth noting at this point that, technically, publishers cannot break their own Conditions of Sale. Booksellers frequently object to the special offers made by publishers (e.g. through magazines, or with packets of breakfast cereal) enabling the public to purchase a net book at below the net price. Whilst it can be argued that this is against the spirit of the NBA, and unfair to the bookseller who has undertaken to sell the book at the higher net price, such offers are not breaches of the NBA; the publisher is at liberty to sell his books at whatever price he likes to whomever he likes, and therefore cannot be said to be breaking the NBA.

Sometimes offers are made with the use of coupons, where the customer takes the coupons to the bookshop and the bookseller accepts payment partly in cash and partly in coupons. This is in order within the Net Book system, the companies providing the coupons being held to be topping up the price, and the market research value of the coupons being regarded as the difference between the net price and the actual amount of cash the purchaser is asked to pay.

Exceptions to the NBA

As mentioned earlier there are instances when a net book may be sold for less than its net price. These exceptions are subject to stringent regulations as laid down in the text of the Net Book Agreement – for a full version of the text, see Appendix 5.

Before explaining the exceptions, it should be said that a book is considered to be sold at less than the net price when any inducements to buy or considerations in kind are offered. This means that a bookseller may not make offers such as 'One free squash ball with every copy of *Complete Squash Rules*' or 'Free £1 book token with every purchase over £10'. He may not offer to provide any service, e.g. library book services (card indexing, stamping, etc.), at less than the cost to himself, although he may offer free postage and packing. This restriction on offers stops one bookseller from inducing the public to buy in his shop rather than his competitor's, which would make a mockery of the system of net prices were it allowed.

There are basically two ways in which a net book may be sold by the bookseller at a discount:

a) with the publisher's permission
b) under the provisions of various licences granted by the Publishers Association

In the first case, booksellers may request permission from the publisher to sell off old or unwanted stock after twelve months have elapsed since the date of the last order placed for those titles by the bookseller. He should offer them back to the publisher at cost, or at the proposed sale price, and only when the publisher has indicated that he does not wish to buy back the stock can the bookseller reduce the price. A bookseller can hold a sale at any time of the year, provided he has met all the above requirements.

Books which have become damaged or shop-soiled are still subject to the NBA. A damaged book may be considered as a second-hand book and these, along with review copies, may be sold at a discount once six months have elapsed since the original date of publication.

From time to time, publishers need to clear their warehouses of slow-moving or unwanted stock. There are several ways of doing this. They can 'de-net' an unwanted title, whereby it remains on their list and they retain an interest in its sale. They also continue to pay the author royalties on the title. Alternatively, they can 'remainder' the book, whereby they decide that they no longer have room for it on their list and sell the entire stock to a remainder dealer who disposes of it to the bookshops. Another option is the National Book Sale. This is an annual event at which booksellers can sell off their slow-moving stock of net titles, but publishers also have the opportunity to put slow-moving stock into the Sale in the hope that booksellers will buy it for resale as a 'special offer'. Outside the period of the National Book Sale, the publisher can 'de-net' in order to allow the bookseller to set his own price, or reduce its price, while keeping it as a net book.

Bookshop staff are allowed to purchase any book at a discount at the shop's discretion, as they are classed as members of the trade rather than as members of the public.

The second set of exceptions to the NBA are the various

licences enabling institutions, and in some cases individuals, to purchase net books at a discount.

1 The Library Licence

Libraries may apply to the PA for a licence to purchase books at not more than a 10% discount, provided they allow free access to the public – they need not provide lending facilities but the public must be able to use the library for reference. This means that all public libraries qualify for a licence, as do college libraries, which are prepared to grant free access and spend a minimum of £100 per annum on new net books (although some school libraries agree to receive their books on loan from a public library, thereby indirectly enjoying the benefit of the library licence discount).

The library must state on its application the names of booksellers who wish to supply it at discount, and no-one but the named booksellers may do so. Where a bookseller has received less than 20.84% discount on a purchase from a publisher, he is not obliged to offer the library its usual 10% discount. (See Appendix 6.)

2 The Primary and Secondary School Licence

Operating in a similar fashion to the Library Licence, the Primary and Secondary School Licence allows the licensee a discount on purchases of net books from willing booksellers.

The licensee must be either a primary or secondary school, teaching a full curriculum to full-time students, and must be recognised by the appropriate authorities, or may be a local education authority responsible for such schools. Colleges of further education, universities and other institutions for tertiary education do not qualify.

The school or education authority applies to the Publisher's Association for the licence, and a copy of the licence must then be lodged with each supplying bookseller. The bookseller is then permitted, but not required, to grant a discount of up to 10% on net books purchased through the licence.

3 Book Agent's Licence

A licence may be granted to individuals who run bookstalls in places such as churches or schools, or wherever books are not normally available for purchase. The book agent must ensure that the books are sold to the end consumer at the full net price, and the licence granted by the PA authorises a nominated bookseller to supply the bookstall at a discount of up to half the discount received from the publisher. The books supplied must always be for resale, and not for the use of the institution itself.

Occasionally school bookshops (and other similar arrangements) do not operate under an official Book Agent's Licence, but may receive a small discount from the supplying bookseller as a commission for making sales on the bookseller's behalf. Once again, the books must be intended for resale at the full net price, and because the PA has not seen involved in granting a licence, the responsibility for ensuring that the NBA is observed remains with the bookseller (see Appendix 7).

4 Service Unit Library Licence

HM Forces service units, who may not have access to a bookshop or library, can apply to the PA for a licence authorising a named bookseller to supply them at a 10% discount. The discount was increased to 10% from 7.5%, which had been the fixture for many years, in 1989. Books purchased must be solely for use in the unit library. The costs of any ancillary services (such as card-indexing, jacketing, etc.) must not be charged at less than their actual cost to the bookseller.

5 Quantity Book Buying Licence

This licence is granted to cover a single purchase of a large quantity of net books, for primarily philanthropic purposes (for example, a company wishing to buy a number of books as gifts for an overseas trade delegation, or a commercial body wishing to set up a staff library). Discount is allowed on a sliding scale from 5%–10% on orders worth £250-£750 and more for assorted titles, or a flat rate of 10% is allowed for an order of twelve or more copies of one title, provided the total value is over £25. The bookseller wishing to offer a quantity book buying discount applies to the PA, and the licence granted is valid for only the one specified transaction (see Appendix 8).

Changes in Price

One further area which is often a source of confusion to both booksellers and the public is what happens when a publisher changes the price of a book. If a price is lowered (when a title is remaindered, for example), the publisher should credit the bookseller for the difference between the old and new price for the copies he still has in stock. When the price is raised, the bookseller is not bound automatically to increase his stock accordingly, but may continue to sell at the old net price (as would have been shown on the original invoice).

However, publishers frequently increase prices half-way through print runs and supply their books with new price stickers covering the old price. Understandably, the public are prone to peel off such stickers and demand to purchase the book at the lower price, believing that such re-pricing procedures are illegal (as indeed they are for goods not subject to r.p.m.). The bookseller, having been invoiced at the new price, would be breaking the NBA if he were to accede to the customer's wishes and would also, of course, incur a loss of profit. When faced with an irate customer who is convinced he knows his rights as a consumer, all the bookseller can do is gently explain the NBA and r.p.m., or ultimately point him in the direction of his local Consumers Association.

Book Clubs

Having read about the Net Book Agreement, you may well be wondering how it is that book clubs can offer new titles at discounted prices.

The answer is that the sale of books by this method is very closely controlled by the Publishers Association, who maintain a register of book clubs and are responsible for the Regulations for the Conduct of Book Clubs. This is a set of rules by which both publishers supplying book clubs and the clubs themselves must abide.

The rules state (in brief) that:

1 The book club shall maintain a register of its members.
2 There shall be a minimum period of membership of not less than six months;
3 Club members shall be required to purchase a minimum of three books in the first year of membership;
4 Book clubs may only supply their books to their registered members, and the special offers (known as premiums) made as an inducement to join may only be made to members at the time of applying.

Publishers also have to follow a set of rules and guidelines which mainly determine how many copies of trade edition they may sell to a book club and when.

1 They may not offer a title as a premium until six months have elapsed since its publication as a trade edition (i.e. available to booksellers, etc.);
2 Book club titles must show that they are such by having the club colophon printed on the title page, jacket and binding, except when there is an inadequate supply of the club edition (when the trade edition may be supplied up to a maximum number of copies equal to 20% of the original club order), or when the book club does not have exclusive rights to the title (when the publisher will be allowed to supply up to 5000 copies or 50% of the original print run for that title, whichever is lower).

The rules are fairly lengthy and complex, but their existence should reassure you that book clubs are not free to offer anything and everything to whomever they wish. The PA and BA liaise over the regulations, ensuring that the interests of retail booksellers are taken into consideration.

There are also clauses included which help to protect the bookseller from appearing in an unfavourable light compared to book clubs: the clubs' advertising blurb is subject to control, and any bookseller who feels that a club is making statements which may be detrimental to bookshops can register a complaint with the Publishers Association.

In general, the aim of the book club regulations is to achieve control with 'the minimum degree required for the purpose', and to safeguard the interests of the public. The official view as expressed in the opening paragraphs of the regulations is that 'book clubs have a valuable function to perform in the publication and distribution of books', and whilst it is true that this opinion is often the subject of hot debate, it can be argued that book clubs can help to promote books to a section of the public who may not or cannot visit bookshops regularly. They may also play a part in encouraging people to read, thereby developing a book-buying habit which could ultimately bring customers to your bookshop, in search of a wider selection than is available through their club.

Copies of the full text of the regulations are available from the Publishers Association.

There are, however, further pieces of legislation pertaining to books with which you should be familiar. It is unlikely in fact that you will need to understand such law down to the last detail as much of it concerns publishers more directly, but it is as well to know it exists. Indeed, in the last few years there have been several well-publicised cases where booksellers have run into legal complications when selling titles which have been the subject of copyright and libel actions, so it is a good idea at least to be aware of the possible implications of this very specialised legislation.

Law of Copyright

Copyright is essentially a property right, a legal method of ensuring that the ownership of a creative work resides with its creator, be it a work of art, music or the written word (amongst other things). Its purpose is to guarantee the author due recognition for his work, so that he can receive accurate financial remuneration, and to prevent misuse or abuse of his creation. This being the case, the author can ascribe or transfer the rights to another party, either in whole or in part. The terms used are 'to license', and 'to assign' copyright, and as anyone who has ever seen an author/-publisher contract will know, the whole matter is legally very complex.

Whether it is the author or the publisher who holds copyright, the main effect of this law is to prevent the copying, reproducing, transmitting or electronic storing of copyright material without the holder's permission. Where an author retains copyright, this is valid for fifty years after the death of the author, and then work is said to 'come out of copyright'. A recent example of an author's works becoming available for publication by anyone is that of Beatrix Potter, where not only are new editions of her books now available, but also a whole range of other merchandise inspired by her characters.

In general, copyright law is observed internationally, with two conventions (the Berne Convention and the Universal Copyright Convention) providing protection overseas for authors. However, the Publishers Association has a continual battle on its hands to prevent what is known as piracy, where publishers in certain countries persist in reproducing books for their own markets with no acknowledgement or payment to the copyright holder.

Obscenity, Libel and Official Secrets

Under the Obscene Publications Act, publishing is defined as the complete act of making public, and therefore includes printing, distribution, selling or offering for sale, giving and lending. It therefore follows that booksellers are liable to prosecution for offering for sale any item which is deemed to be obscene, profane and so on.

Apart from the Obscene Publications Act, there also exist a variety of other laws which control what may or may not be sold in the form of printed matter.These include the Defamation Act, the Indecent Displays Act, The Post Office Act (which prohibits the sending through the post of any such material) and the Children & Very Young Persons (Harmful Publications) Act (which controls the sale to young persons of stories which pictorially depict violence, pornography, etc.). It is also illegal to import such literature, which can be seized by HM Customs, under the Customs Consolidation Act.

In general, you will probably be able to recognise anything which could be termed an offensive publication, and can then make up your own mind as to whether or not you should stock it. The greyer legal areas, however, cover defamation and libel, or books containing information covered by the Official Secrets Act. There have been several well-publicised cases recently, such as Robert Maxwell's attempts to prevent publication of suspected defamatory biographies of himself, and the Government's suppression of Peter Wright's memoirs *Spycatcher*.

In both instances, booksellers were informed that to offer these titles for sale could lead to prosecution, therefore they continued to sell at their own risk. In most cases, the publishers of such books act responsibly and will recall stocks from booksellers if they suspect that publication may lead to legal action.

You should also be aware that books exist dealing with other subjects whose practices are deemed to be outside the law. Booksellers should take care, for example, when offered titles on topics such as pit bull terriers, which may well include the illegal activities of dog-fighting, badger-baiting, and so on. With such sensitive areas, it could well be an irate animal-loving customer who reports you to the authorities.

Law for Retailers

As mentioned earlier, if you are setting up your own bookshop you will also need to familiarise yourself with laws and regulations relating to you trading as a company, and to you as an employer. If you are working in a bookshop, you will at least need to understand basic consumer law: failure to do so could result in a prosecution being brought against the shop by the Offices of Fair Trading, local Trading Standards Officers or by a customer who takes out a civil action.

However, all the above areas of law are common to all employment, trading and retailing operations, and there are plenty of books and other sources of advice to help you ensure that your activities are within the law.

10

The Trade Organisations

One of the things often said in favour of the book trade is that it is still a remarkably small world, a friendly trading environment where everyone knows everybody else. However one views it, the fact remains that the various component parts of the trade do liaise closely with one another and generally communicate in an amiable and constructive manner, probably due to sharing a common aim, which is to sell more books.

Apart from personal contact within the trade at events such as book fairs and seminars, and between publishers' sales staff and booksellers, formal discussion and communication is mainly conducted through the trade organisations, such as the Booksellers, Publishers and Library Associations, and other bodies. Whilst it is perhaps not essential that you understand all the aims and functions of all these parties, it will undoubtedly be helpful for you to have some idea of their various areas of responsibility.

The Booksellers Association

The BA was set up in 1895 to 'protect and promote the interests of booksellers'. The Association currently has approximately 3400 bookshops in membership, ranging in size from the large multiples such as W. H. Smith to tiny one-man businesses with an annual turnover of only a few thousand pounds.

The work carried out by the BA on behalf of its members ranges from lobbying politicians in Westminster and Brussels through to asking publishers to revise the formats of their invoices. In addition, the BA also provides a variety of services, including training programmes, advice on marketing, computerisation, shop design, etc., and it produces stationery and publications for everyday use. We shall look at these services in greater detail further on.

How Does It Function?

The BA itself has a permanent staff, headed by a Director. The bulk of the work carried out is determined by various committees and the BA's governing body, its Council. Major policy decisions are agreed upon at the Annual General Meeting which is held during the Annual Conference, and the elected Council and committee members then decide how best to implement these.

Apart from the central organisation, the BA also has 15 regional branches. Each branch is run by its own elected officers and committee, and meets regularly to monitor and discuss book trade activities at a local level, and arrange local training sessions. The branches also fulfill a social function, bringing together booksellers from all over the region and maintaining contact with the centre of activity in London.

A representative from each of the branches sits on the Council, together with members elected at the AGM. The Council is headed by the President, who holds office for two years and is aided by Officers – the immediate Past President, the Vice-President and the Honorary Treasurer. It meets regularly to discuss events, decide upon necessary action and receive reports from the various committees which account directly to it. Each committee is responsible for a different book trade area; they are as follows:

The Finance & General Purposes Committee (F & GP)

Administers the finance for both the daily running of the BA and the funding of various projects carried out by the Association.

The Trade Practice & Distribution Committee

Acts as a watchdog committee, protecting members' interests in legal, political and general trade matters, liaising with publishers and the PA.

The Marketing Committee
Helps booksellers actively to market and promote their shops and services, and is also involved in helping to promote books and reading to the public, liaising with other bodies involved in this area.

The Training Committee
Identifies the trade's training and educational requirements; administers the Certificate in Bookselling Skills and a variety of one-day and residential training courses.

The Standing Committee on Technology
Monitors technological developments which may affect booksellers. Also looks at matters at international and inter-trade levels, advising on guidelines and standards for trade technology.

Specialist Groups
Apart from these specific committees, booksellers who share a common trading interest (e.g. export booksellers, religious booksellers, etc.) have formed groups which act as forums for discussion for matters specifically relating to their type of bookselling. These specialist groups elect executive committees and hold their own AGMs at which policy decisions are made, reports of the group's activities over the past year are given and elections are held.

The groups are as follows:

The Religious Booksellers Group
The Charter Group
The Library Booksellers Group
The School Suppliers Group
The Export Booksellers Group
The Wholesalers Group
The College & University Booksellers Group
The Childrens Booksellers Group

Probably all of the above interests are self-explanatory, with the exception of the Charter Group. The Charter Group was set up in 1964 with the aim of encouraging excellence and professionalism in bookselling. To qualify for membership of the Group, a bookshop must meet certain criteria. Amongst these are requirements concerning minimum stockholding value, commitment to staff training, obligation to provide a customer order service and to produce annual financial accounts for analysis by the Manchester Business School as data for the Charter Economic Survey (see p.152). Charter booksellers, in return for their commitment to professionalism, may enjoy higher discounts from certain publishers, known as Charter bonus terms.

Other BA committees include the Conference Committee, which makes plans for the organisation and events at the Annual Conference, and the Open University Set Books Stockists Scheme Committee, which is set up in order to help booksellers who choose to become part of this scheme.

Other Groups and Working Parties

BA members and staff also sit on many other committees and councils, often run in liaison with other book trade associations. A full list of the membership of these can be found at the end of the BA Annual Report. They include:

The Teleordering Users' Council

A forum for both publisher and bookseller users of the Teleordering system, at which political issues, service problems and improvements are discussed with representatives of Teleordering Ltd.

The Machine Readable Codes Working Party

A body set up to establish guidelines for the production and use of bar codes in the book trade. Members include booksellers, publishers, librarians and printers.

The National Book Sale Committee

Organises an annual sale in which publishers and booksellers can sell off their overstocks and unwanted titles at reduced prices. Representatives of both the PA and the BA are responsible for the running of the sale.

In addition to the work carried out by these particular groups and committees, the BA comes into contact with a host of other organisations in the course of its daily work. The BA in turn belongs to associations, such as GALC (the European association of booksellers' associations), the National Chamber of Trade, and the Trade and Professional Alliance. It liaises with the banks and credit card companies, lawyers and government departments – in short, it speaks to anyone who might have an interest in either bookselling or retailing in general, or whose activities might have an effect on BA members.

BA Services

As mentioned earlier, apart from looking after members' interests in a political and diplomatic function, the BA is involved in providing schemes and products to make members' lives easier and to help them improve their profitability. The Association wholly owns three other companies – Book Tokens Ltd, Book Trade Improvement Ltd and the Booksellers Association Service House Ltd.

Book Tokens Ltd

Book Tokens Ltd was founded in 1932, and is today the most widely used of the Association's services. Book tokens may only be sold by members of the BA. The scheme operates as follows.

Booksellers order a selection of special book token stamps and cards from the company, which they sell in their shop. Customers then choose how much they want to give, and token stamps amounting to that value are fixed to the special card. A wide variety of card designs is available and the cost of the card goes wholly to Book Tokens Ltd to administer the scheme. The book token can then be exchanged in any participating bookshop in the country. Booksellers accept book tokens at their full face value in either part or whole payment for books, and may not give change in cash for a partly used token (although it is recommended that they use common sense and discretion with regard to the last few pence unspent). It is usual to offer either a shop credit note or another book token as change when the books purchased do not amount to the full value of the original token.

Booksellers' accounts with Book Tokens Ltd are settled quarterly; the books of stamps have serial numbers which are logged against the bookseller's account, so that Book Tokens Ltd know exactly how much stock a company has purchased. Booksellers return the redeemed book tokens, and a discount of 12.5% is deducted from the face value and credited to the bookseller who originally sold the stamp, leaving the redeeming bookseller 87.5% of the stamp's value. In fact, compared with the total value of transactions made via book tokens, relatively little money changes hands at the quarterly settlements as a sort of 'rolling-stock' situation occurs, with booksellers' purchases of stamps equalling the remuneration from exchanging them. The stamps are only paid for when sold, and a statement of account is rendered quarterly.

Book tokens are of great value to booksellers in generating extra sales. They achieve this in a variety of ways:

a) Schools and other institutions like to give book tokens as prizes and gifts where they might not be prepared to spend the same amount on a book or selection of books.
b) Customers like to give book tokens as gifts when they are unsure of the recipient's taste or personal book collection. They are also ideal gifts for sending long-distance.
c) Recipients of book tokens will often make extra purchases above the value of their token.

Further, book tokens are an ideal way of getting people into bookshops who may not be regular visitors – anything which encourages reading and book-buying habits is beneficial to booksellers.

Book Trade Improvement Ltd

Owned by Book Tokens Ltd, Book Trade Improvement Ltd exists to make financial loans to BA members who wish to improve their shops. Funds are available for shop refits, renovations and some equipment installations (e.g. computer systems, etc.)

BASH

The BA Service House was set up in 1977 to handle the Association's trading operations. All BA services available (other than those covered by Book Tokens Ltd and Book Trade Improvement Ltd) fall into BASH's area of responsibility. The following is a brief guide to BASH's services.

Marketing Aids

Initiated by the Marketing Committee, BA Marketing produces a variety of items to help the bookseller promote his bookshop and a wide range of new books to his customers. These include:

Promotional Calender, which lists key book trade and general arts events throughout the year, helping booksellers to plan promotional campaigns tying in with these.

BA Christmas Catalogue This is a full-colour illustrated selection of books for Christmas, intended for either door-to-door or point-of-sale distribution. The bookseller can have the name of his shop overprinted on the cover, and the catalogue also includes a free competition for customers. Further catalogues, such as Summer Reading and the Business Books Catalogue, are produced from time to time.

Help in Cutting Costs

A variety of services exists to help booksellers maximise their profits and streamline their daily routines:

The Booksellers Clearing House (BCH), owned by Book Tokens Ltd, enables booksellers to simplify their accounting procedures by acting as a central clearing house for payment of publishers' invoices. Booksellers can settle all their payments by one cheque, thereby reducing bank charges and office work.

The Small Order Giro Scheme works with the National Girobank to help booksellers avoid small order surcharges and time-wasting pro forma invoices. Booksellers open an account with the National Girobank, and can purchase from the BA specially produced four-part Giro order forms, which combine the functions of cheque and order form (see p.28). The forms are overprinted with the bookseller's name and when completed and sent to a publisher, act as a 'cash with order'.

The **Booksell** scheme is a special contract negotiated between the BA and the Post Office to help reduce the postal charges of those booksellers who regularly send out a large volume of parcels. The preferential contract rates are available to companies who post over 1000 parcels per annum, with extra discounts offered for submission of mail direct to a sorting office.

The BA also produces **standard stationery** for booksellers – stock control cards, stock and single copy order forms, returns and query forms are all supplied for use in communicating with publishers.

Other schemes which the BA helps to run include **Post-a-Book** (a special mailing service set up by the Post Office in conjunction with the BA and PA enabling customers to purchase and post a book in one transaction in the bookshop), and the **National Book Sale**.

The **Whitbread Literary Awards** (worth a total of £29,000 in

1989) are administered by the BA, who organise promotional point-of-sale material for the winning titles for bookshops.

Training

The Association recognises that training and education are of key importance in the running of profitable, successful bookshops and in the promotion of books to the public. To this end, it holds one-day and residential training courses for booksellers at all levels in their careers, covering subjects as diverse as practice and theory of window display through to finance for managers. The main qualification for the trade is the BA Certificate in Bookselling Skills, an open learning course which had recently been revised and updated to meet the recommendations of the Government's National Council for Vocational Qualifications. Advice is also given on how to make the most of the various training grants and bursaries available. A leaflet on starting a career is available from the BA Training Department, who will be glad to answer any queries on the content of and enrolment on CIBS.

BA Publications

The publication of facts and information forms a major part of the services the BA provides for its members and to the trade as a whole. A wide range of leaflets is available explaining trade regulations to interested parties such as schools and libraries, and covering published trade guidelines and standards for booksellers. Many of these are free, although there is a nominal charge for some. However, probably the most important and most widely used of the BA publications are those which are produced annually (prices quoted are obviously subject to alteration):

The BA Directory of Members One copy available free of charge to each corporate member, otherwise £17.00. Includes names and addresses of all bookshops in membership, listed both geographically and alphabetically. Also gives Head Office addresses, with locations of shop branches. Each entry shows the bookshop's subject specialisations, services provided, membership of BA specialist groups, BA branch membership, and shop manager's name.

The BA Directory of Publishers & Wholesalers £23.00 to members, otherwise £33.00. Lists names and addresses of over 4000 publishers and distributors in the UK and Ireland, including the distribution arrangements for overseas publishers whose books are available here. Each entry lists full communications details, key personnel, types of books published and trade terms. Also included are full details of over 90 wholesalers stating stock carried and services provided, as well as suppliers of spoken word cassettes. A list of useful addresses appears at the front of the Directory, with a list of names and addresses of over 30 remainder dealers at the back.

The BA Annual Report Free to members. Gives an account of the major work and achievements carried out by the Association over the past year. Reports from Council, the committees and branches are included, and an account of the BA finances also appears. At the end of the report is a full list showing membership of all committees and BA involvements in working parties, etc. outside the Association.

The Charter Group Economic Survey £40.00. One of the requirements for membership of the Charter Group is the submission of annual trading figures for analysis. The Manchester Business School annually examines and reports on Charter booksellers' accounts, producing invaluable tables of statistics with full commentaries, enabling booksellers to compare their own performance with that of others. The Economic Survey gives the most complete picture of the true economics of book retailing today.

Book Retailing in the 1990s £25.00 to members, £40.00 to non-members. In 1987 the BA commissioned the Arthur Young group of business consultants to prepare a report projecting the state of book retailing in the next decade, based on the current situation and trends both in and around the market. The set of conclusions and recommendations are essential reading for anyone expecting to be selling books in five year's time, and form a major part of the Association's objectives and considerations for the future.

The BA Bookshop Computer Guide £8.00 to members, £12.00 to non-members. A guide intended to help you assess your requirements from a computer system, choose the right one, purchase and install it. Overviews of current book trade technological developments which may be of benefit to you, plus comprehensive details of bookshop software are included, along with lists of suppliers and manufacturers, and further sources of advice.

The BPRA Handbook £5.00. A complete listing of the names and addresses of members of the Book Publishers Representatives

Association, also showing which geographical regions and which publishers are covered by each representative.

Bookselling News Free to members. The official journal of the BA, *Bookselling News* is published approximately five times per year, and aims to update the members with the Association's activities, and any other issues which may affect booksellers (e.g. changes in legislation, etc.). Occasional articles are contributed from both members and individuals, such as security specialists, computer systems suppliers, etc.

The BA publishes a range of other titles, some covering specific topics such as *How to Improve School Book Supplies – A Teacher's Guide* and *The Economic Implications of the NBA*. A price list giving all details of publications is available on request.

The Publishers Association

The PA's role is similar to that of the BA in that it exists to promote the interests of its members, and seeks to maintain a climate which will encourage a healthy publishing industry. Again, like the BA, the PA maintains a permanent staff headed by a Chief Executive and is controlled by an elected Council, aided by committees responsible for specific areas. The basic annual subscription to the PA gives members access to its 'core' services, with further optional services available for an extra subscription. These are:

The Educational Publishers Council
The EPC looks after the interests of school book publishers, and aims to ensure adequate provision of books in schools. It liaises with the Government, schools, local authorities, etc.

The University, College and Professional Publishers Council
UCPPC co-ordinates the activities of those involved in academic book publishing, liaising with bodies involved in higher education and the professions, organising exhibitions at conferences, etc.

The Book Development Council
The aim of the BDC is to expand overseas markets by liaising with international bodies, organising overseas exhibitions and working closely with the British Council.

Apart from these specific roles the PA, like the BA, is involved in lobbying governments both at home and abroad on matters such as VAT, copyright law and other legislation. The PA also, most importantly, acts as guardian of the Net Book Agreement (see p 171). Publisher members of the PA do not necessarily have to be signatories of the NBA (i.e. bound to publish their books at fixed 'net' prices), but those who are must undertake to ensure that its conditions are observed.

The PA carries out work via many joint trade committees, liaising frequently with both the BA and the Library Association, etc. It produces a range of publications of interest to publishers and the rest of the trade, one of the most important of which, *The Book Trade Yearbook*, is published annually by the PA Statistics Collection Service.

This gives a complete breakdown of the output and sales of the books produced, price indices and comments and analysis of the market as a whole.

Book Trust

The main aim of Book Trust (formerly known as the National Book League) is to 'promote the role of books in society', which it does by making books and reading more accessible to people. It provides a variety of services, such as offering bibliographic information, book guides and a reference library for children's books, and initiates research projects and helps in the co-ordination of book trade campaigns. Probably its most noted activity is the administration of the annual Booker Prize (awarded for fiction), although it is also responsible for many other literary awards, such as the Thomas Cook Travel & Guide Book awards and the Smarties Prize for children's books.

The Children's Book Foundation

This comes under the aegis of Book Trust, and is a separate division aimed at promoting children's use of books.

Book House Training Centre

A charitable educational trust set up by Sir Stanley Unwin, BHTC provides training primarily for those employed in publishing, but also works alongside the BA Training Department and organises an annual Joint Seminar for Publishers and Booksellers, aimed at those who have recently joined the book trade. Each year the Unwin Foundation Travelling Scholarship is awarded to a young person from any part of the trade, enabling him or her to pursue a relevant research project.

The Library Association

The LA looks after the interests of libraries and professional librarians. It sponsors research in library activities, and publishes books and papers on the subject. It is also responsible for examining and awarding the two professional qualifications in the field, Associate and Fellow of the LA.

The Society of Young Publishers

The SYP provides a lively forum for discussion for young people working in publishing. Meetings are held regularly, with guest speakers tackling topics relevant to the industry.

The Society of Authors

This professional association offers help and advice to authors on legal matters (such as copyright, contracts, etc.) and seeks to promote the professional status and rights of authors in all related areas.

The Independent Publishers Guild

The IPG is an association which exists to aid and promote the interests of independent publishers. Many of its members are small publishing companies who do not belong to the PA, although some belong to both bodies, and houses as large and prestigious as Macmillan are also in membership. The IPG provides a sort of co-operative forum to meet the needs of independent publishers, helping with the sharing of exhibition stands, advertising, etc.

The Book Publishers Representatives Association

The BPRA is the forum for the exchange of information concerning the services offered by publishers' representatives. It maintains a benevolent fund for distressed members and produces an employment register for publishers seeking representational services.

The International Booksellers Federation

This is the international body of booksellers' associations, to which most associations in Western Europe and the English-speaking countries belong. An annual IBF Conference is held at which members' concerns and opinions are openly discussed. Sponsored by the IBF is the ICYB – the *International Congress of Young Booksellers*. This group also holds an annual conference, which takes as its theme for discussion a topic of interest to all member nations (e.g. technology in the book trade, training and education of booksellers, etc.).

The addresses of most of these trade bodies can be found in Appendix 3 at the end of this book. Regular reading of the trade press, and in particular any journals or periodicals produced by these associations, will help you to become more familiar with their activities (a list of trade journals is in Appendix 2).

You may also come across references to further groups and committees in your reading; many will in fact be inter-trade working parties whose representatives are drawn from one or more of the above mentioned bodies, such as MUG (the MARC User Group), BEDIS (the Book trade Electronic Data Interchange Systems Committee), and BTECC (Book Trade Electronic Communications Committee). Further information concerning the activities of such groups can usually be obtained from one of the main trade associations.

Appendix 1

Annual Book Trade Events

There are many regular book trade events and promotions which may be of interest either to you or your customers, some of which may provide a focus for displays and sales campaigns within your bookshop.

Literary Awards

There are literally hundreds of literary prizes awarded each year, although only a handful receive enough publicity to capture the attention of the average customer in the street.

Probably the two best known are the Booker Prize and the Whitbread Literary Award, the first being for an outstanding novel and the second being divided into the categories of first novel, poetry, biography, children's book and novel, with an overall winner. Both award ceremonies are usually televised and attract much media attention.

There are also several important awards for children's books (such as the Smarties Prize), for travel writing (the Thomas Cook Travel Award) and for first novels – in the case of children's books these may attract the attention of schools or playgroup customers.

Book Fairs

The purpose of the main international book fairs is primarily the buying and selling of rights for books, and because of this they are more likely to be of interest to publishers than to booksellers. They include the well-established Frankfurt Book Fair (now in its 41st year), the Bologna (for children's books), Cairo, Moscow and Beijing Book Fairs, and many others. The London International Book Fair, held annually in the Spring, is increasing in popularity and is visited by many booksellers and those interested in the trade. It is a good place to get the feel of the British publishing scene, and to become familiar with the output of the various publishers present. Useful trade contracts can also be made with publishers, remainder dealers and computer systems suppliers.

Of equal interest to booksellers is the BA Trade Exhibition, held on one day during the BA Annual Conference. A wide range of trade exhibitors are present, frequently offering extra discounts for orders placed at the exhibition.

Book Festivals

Many regional arts associations organise local arts and book festivals throughout the year, and there may be an opportunity for your bookshop to participate.

Other major festivals which receive publicity are Children's Book Week (organised by the Children's Book Foundation), the Edinburgh Book Festival and Feminist Book Fortnight. Depending on the location or specialisation of your shop, you may well be able to tie in with the attention these attract.

Appendix 2

Book Trade Journals

The following book trade journals may be of interest, and can be valuable reference tools:

The Bookseller
12 Dyott Street, London WC1A 1DF (071–836 8911). Weekly; subscription £67 pa, or £1.15 per issue. Contains news of trade events, company news, book reviews plus advertisements, features and reports and Whitaker's 'Publications of the Week'.

Publishing News
43 Museum Street, London WC1A 1LY (071–404 0304). Weekly; subscription £45 pa. Of interest to both publishers and booksellers; trade news, features, plus previews and books receiving media coverage.

The Radical Bookseller
265 Seven Sisters Road, London N4 2DE (081–802 8773). 10 issues pa; subscription £15 pa, £10 pa to small shops and publishers. Carries news of radical publications and events.

Bookselling News
154 Buckingham Palace Road, London SWIW 9TZ (071–730 8214). Approx 5 issues pa; free to BA members, £20 pa to non-members. The official newsletter of the Booksellers Association.

The European Christian Bookseller Review (incorporating *Christian Bookseller Update*)
c/o The Association of Christian Booksellers of Gt Britain and Europe, Grampian House, 144 Deansgate, Manchester M3 3EE (061–835 3000). Published monthly; free to members of the Association, otherwise £18 pa. The official journal of the Association of Christian Booksellers of Gt Britain and Europe.

The European Bookseller
2 Vale Court, 28 Maida Vale, London W9 1RT (071–289 4247). Published monthly, plus occasional special features issues; £36 pa. The European trade journal for the English language book trade.

Books in the Media
Bookwatch Ltd, 15 Up East Street, Lewin's Yard, Chesham, Bucks HP5 1HQ. A weekly checklist of titles covered in the media. £62 for BA/LA members; otherwise £67.50. A bestsellers poster is also available, as is a joint or separate subscription.

Books for Keeps
6 Brightfield Road, Lee, London SE12 8QF (081–852 4953). 6 issues pa; subscription £9.30 pa or £1.55 per issue. The official newsletter of the School Bookshop Association.

Book News (incorporating *CBF News*)
Book Trust, Book House, 45 East Hill, London SW18 2QZ (081–870 9055). Published quarterly; subscription £6 pa. The official journal of Book Trust and the Children's Book Foundation. Carries news of literary award and prizes, regional arts news and forthcoming literary and arts events.

British Book News
c/o Journals Dept, Basil Blackwell, 108 Cowley Road, Oxford OX4 1JF (0865–791155). Published monthly; subscription £30 pa for individuals, £40 pa for institutions (single copies £2.70 and £3.90 respectively). The journal of the British Council, covering literary and educational news both at home and abroad, survey articles, forthcoming books listings and library news.

SYP Inprint
c/o J Whitaker & Son, 12 Dyott Street, London WCIA 1DF (071–836 8911). Monthly; free to members of the SYP. The journal of the Society of Young Publishers. Contains news of seminars and social events, and features on the book trade.

IPG Bulletin
14A Anindel Gardens, London W11 (071–727 8501). 5 issues, pa; free to members. Newsletter of the Independent Publishers Guild, carrying news of members, forthcoming trade events, services offered and reports of IPG seminars.

The Clique
c/o Picaflow Ltd, 7 Pulleyn Drive, York Y02 2DY (0904–31752), Published bi-monthly; subscription cost available on request. The journal for antiquarian and second-hand booksellers.

Quiddity
509 Premier House, Greycoat Place, London SW1P 1SB (071–222 8866 ext. 2553). Published monthly; subscription £50 pa. International review of marketing and new technology for publishers.

There are many other publications which may be of interest to you as a bookseller, depending on your bookshop's areas of specialisation. Many other countries have their own equivalent of *The Bookseller*, which are obviously useful if you are dealing with books from overseas.

Most associations have their own newsletters (e.g. The Publishers Association 'Newslines'), and also the large chains produce company magazines, but none of these is likely to be of much interest to you unless you are directly involved. Also available are periodicals for the news trade (e.g. *Newsagent*).

However, those listed are probably the most widely read amongst booksellers in the UK, and it is certainly advisable to read *The Bookseller* or *Publishing News* regularly to keep in touch with trade developments and information concerning new books and publishing companies.

Appendix 3

Book Trade Organisation Addresses

Antiquarian Booksellers Association
Suite 2
26 Charing Cross Road
London WC2H 0DG
Tel: 071–379 3041

Association of Christian Booksellers of Gt Britain & Europe
Grampian House, 144 Deansgate
Manchester M3 3EE
Tel: 061–835 3000

Book Data
Northumberland House, 2 King Street
Twickenham
Middx TW1 3RZ
Tel: 081–892 2272

Book House Ireland
65 Middle Abbey Street
Dublin 1, Ireland
Tel: 0001–730108

Book Publishers Representatives Association
3 Carolina Way
Tiptree
Essex C05 0DW
Tel: 0621–816710

Book Trade Benevolent Society
Dillon Lodge
The Retreat
Kings Langley
Hertfordshire WD4 8LT
Tel: 09277–63128

Book Trust
Book House
45 East Hill
Wandsworth
London SW18 2QZ
Tel: 081–870 9055/8
Also Book House Training Centre and Children's Book Foundation

Book Trust of Scotland,
15A Lynedoch Street,
Glasgow G3 6EF
Tel: 041–332 0391

The Booksellers Association
154 Buckingham Palace Road
London SW1W 9TZ
Tel: 071–730 8214/5/6
Also Book Tokens Ltd, Book Trade Improvement Ltd and Booksellers Clearing House
From late 1990, the new address will be: 154 Vauxhall Bridge Road, London SWIV 1BA.

Christian Booksellers Convention
41F Dace Road
London E3 2NG
Tel: 081–986 0178

Edinburgh Book Festival
25A South West Thistle Street Lane
Edinburgh EH2 1EW
Tel: 031–225 1915

Federation of Radical Booksellers
c/o Housmans Bookshop
5 Caledonian Road
London N1 9DX

Independent Publishers Guild
147–149 Gloucester Terrace
London W2 6DX
Tel: 071–723 7328

International Book Development Ltd
10 Barley Mow Passage
London W4
Tel: 081–944 6477

Irish Book Publishers Association
Book House Ireland
65 Middle Abbey Street
Dublin 1
Tel: 0001–730108

ISSN Agency
UK National Serials Data Centre
British Library
2 Sheraton Street
London W1V 4BH
Tel: 071–323 7159

Library Association
7 Ridgmount Street
London WC1E 7AE
Tel: 071–636 7543

London International Book Fair
Oriel House
26 The Quadrant
Richmond
Surrey TW9 1DL
Tel: 081–940 6065

Music Publishers' Association Ltd
Kingsway House
103 Kingsway
London WC2B 6QX
Tel: 071–831 7591

Periodical Publishers Association
Imperial House
15–19 Kingsway
London WC2B 6UN
Tel: 071–379 6268

The Publishers Association
(inc. BMC, etc.)
19 Bedford Square
London WC1B 3HJ
Tel: 071–580 6321/5

School Bookshop Association/Books for Keeps
6 Brightfield Road
Lee
London SE12 8QF
Tel: 081–852 4953

School Library Association
Liden Library
Barrington Close
Liden
Swindon
Wiltshire SN3 6HF
Tel: 0793–617838

Scottish Publishers Association
25A South West Thistle Street Lane
Edinburgh EH2 1EW
Tel: 031–225 5795

Society of Authors
84 Drayton Gardens
London SW10 9SB
Tel: 071–373 6642

Society of Young Publishers
c/o 12 Dycott Street
London WC1A 1DF
Tel: 071–836 8911

Teleordering Ltd
Wellington House
61–73 Staines Road West
Sunbury-on-Thames
Middlesex TW16 7AH
Tel: 0932–781266

Union of Welsh Publishers and Booksellers
c/o Gomer Press
Llandysul
Dyfed SA44 4BQ
Tel: 055932–2371

Video Trade Association
54D High Street
Northwood
Middlesex HA6 1BL
Tel: 09274–29122

J Whitaker & Sons Ltd
12 Dyott Street
London WC1A 1DF
Tel: 071–836 8911
Also Standard Book Numbering Agency Ltd

Women in Bookselling
c/o Silver Moon Women's Bookshop
68 Charing Cross Road
London WC2H 0BB
Tel: 071–836 7906

Women in Publishing
c/o 12 Dyott Street
London WC1A 1DF

Appendix 4

Book Tokens Limited – Rules and Instructions

Definition of the Scheme

The Book Token Scheme is a scheme whereby members of the public can purchase from a bookseller (the issuing bookseller) Tokens which will be accepted by him or by any other bookseller (the exchanging bookseller) as valid in exchange for books to the full value of the amount indicated by a stamp or stamps on the Token Card.

1 A scheme for members only

Only booksellers who are Members of the Booksellers Association of Great Britain and Ireland are eligible to participate in the Scheme; but the Company reserves the right to refuse Tokens to any bookseller without giving any reason for such refusal and irrespective of his eligibility for participation in the scheme by virtue of membership of the Booksellers Association of Great Britain and Ireland or otherwise. In order to be regarded as a participator a member must agree to sell and exchange Tokens throughout the year.

2 Orders for Token Cards

Token Cards issued by Book Tokens Limited (hereinafter called 'the Company') are sold firm to booksellers. The Company may at any time alter the terms or price at which Token Cards are sold to booksellers.

Booksellers must order Token Cards in multiples of ten. Minimum post free order 30 cards.

3 Net price of Token Card

The bookseller must charge such price as may be laid down from time to time by the Company for each Token Card sold. Failure to do so may disqualify the bookseller from participation in the Book Token Scheme. (*See also Rule 11*).

4 **Value of Token Stamps**
Token Stamps are supplied in denominations of 50p, £1, £2, £5, £10, £20, or such other values as may from time to time be agreed upon by the Company.

5 **Method of Issue**
The issuing bookseller must fill in particulars on the Token Card and affix the stamp in accordance with the following instructions:–

a) The name and address of the issuing bookseller must be printed, written or stamped in the space indicated on the back of the Token Card.
b) The Token Stamp affixed by the issuing bookseller must not be marked in any way by him.
c) More than one stamp may be affixed to one Token Card to make up a composite price, but care should be used in positioning stamps in specially marked areas to leave the serial numbers clearly visible, and stamps should not be stuck on each other.
d) It is not sufficient to pin or clip the stamps to the card.

6 **Stamps on sale or return**
Token Stamps are supplied on sale or return to booksellers whose application to open an account has been approved by the Company. In all other cases they are supplied for cash. **Stamps on sale or return remain the property of the Company but must be paid for if lost**. The right to receive stamps on sale or return may be withdrawn if in the opinion of the Directors of the Company the bookseller's transactions become unsatisfactory; he will then be supplied with stamps only for cash less the discount ruling at the date of purchase. The Directors may at their discretion authorise the recall, collection or inspection of stocks of Token Stamps already supplied on sale or return, and it is a condition of the supply of Token Stamps on sale or return that the bookseller must permit the authorised representative of the Company to inspect or collect stocks of Token Stamps at any time during business hours on being given reasonable notice of his intention to do so.

It is in the common interest that Token Stamps should be placed in the charge of a responsible person and kept in a secure place, and the serial numbers recorded on receipt of stamps from the Company. All stamps and books of stamps should be sold in strictly numerical order. It is recommended that Book Token Stamps be insured against loss by fire or theft and that proper records be kept of transactions so that any such loss can be accurately substantiated.

7 **Cancellation of exchanged stamps**
Tokens presented for exchange should bear complete stamps with the same serial number at both ends. The stamps are automatically cancelled by the bookseller by separating the larger ungummed part of the stamp from the card along the perforation. Booksellers should retain this larger section forwarding to the company (*see Accounts*). The exchanging bookseller should also write or stamp his name and address across the Token Stamps.

In his own interests a bookseller should beware of accepting large numbers of Tokens from unknown persons without verification by the Company.

8 **No time limit**

There is now no time limit on the validity of Book Tokens. **This rule applies to all Tokens** although some earlier cards refer to a period of validity of twelve months or two years.

9 **Lost Tokens**

Tokens lost by members of the public may be replaced only at the discretion of the Company. No claims for such replacements will be entertained until twelve months have elapsed from the time the loss is reported to the Company. No claim for replacement can be considered unless the serial numbers of the last tokens are known.

10 **Official Token Card only**

Token Stamps must be used on the Token Cards issued by the Company. Stamps only, or stamps affixed to any other description of card or paper, are not valid for exchange.

N.B. Any breach of this rule will involve the selling bookseller in a special fee of 20p for every Token so presented for credit.

11 **Book Tokens used as school or library prizes**

When Book Tokens are bought by Schools or Libraries for use as prizes for children, and a certificate is obtained from the Headmaster or Librarian or his accredited representative to the effect that they will be so used, Token Cards may, as a concession, be supplied free of charge, or such concessionary price as the Company may from time to time determine. Booksellers will be credited with the price of cards so supplied on production of the certificate referred to above.

12 **Exchangeable only for books**

Tokens are exchangeable only for books. They may not be exchanged for other goods, or for subscriptions to periodicals. If the bookseller wishes, he may accept Tokens in exchange for second-hand books.

Because various goods have a book-like appearance, construction or description (such as, stamp albums, autograph books etc), we recommend that booksellers should use their discretion and commonsense in accepting customers' Tokens if they choose such goods, rather than become involved in pointless argument.

13 **Not exchangeable for cash**

Tokens may **not** be exchanged for cash.

However because it is difficult always to match the value of a Book Token to the precise cost of the book(s) selected, we recommend to booksellers that they use their discretion and commonsense in the matter of the last few pence unspent, either by giving change or suggesting small stationery items, if stocked, to make up the value.

14 **Accounts**

Booksellers shall account to the Company for sales and exchanges of Tokens in such form and at such periods as shall from time to time be prescribed by the Company. Booksellers who fail to render their accounts within seven days after the second application shall be liable to be regarded as unsatisfactory in their transactions (*see Rule 6*).

The summary and Statement of Account is normally made up four times a year at the following dates: 31st January, 30th April, 31st July, 31st October. The bookseller must complete this in accordance with the instructions thereon and return it without delay to the Company. At each accounting details of stock must be recorded in the space provided, even if no sales have been made during that period. Letters, etc., giving particulars of sales and/or exchanges are not sufficient. Only signed copies of the official Form will be accepted. Additional copies may be had on application to the Company.

15 **Remittance of cash differences**

Where the net value of the Tokens sold plus charges for Cards, etc., exceeds the net value of the Tokens exchanged the difference is due to the Company and the remittance must be sent with the account. Where the net value of Tokens exchanged exceeds that of Tokens sold plus net charges the Company will issue a cheque to the bookseller.

16 **Extra charges**

Booksellers who are not participators in the company's scheme will be charged an additional 7½% discount over and above the 12½% discount due to the issuing booksellers when claiming settlement for Book Tokens exchanged by way of trade. This shall apply both to members and non members of the Booksellers Association of Great Britain and Ireland.

17 **Full value**

The exchanging bookseller is not permitted to deduct from the value of the Book Token any sum by way of compensation for the issuing bookseller's share of discount remitted to the company or for any other reason whatsoever. Customers are entitled to receive a book or books to the full face value of the Book Token.

18 **Return of stamps where business changes hands**

Where a bookselling business ceases to exist or changes hands or goes into liquidation or on the occasion of the death of the proprietor, all unsold stocks of Token Stamps must be returned to the Company if they are held on sale or return. Fresh stocks will not be issued to the successor(s) until confirmation has been obtained from the Booksellers Association of Great Britain and Ireland that transfer of membership has been granted.

19 **Private gift voucher schemes**

Any firm operating a private voucher scheme may also participate in the scheme operated by Book Tokens Ltd, subject to their co-operation as follows:–

a) The word 'token' shall not be used in connection with the operation of any private scheme, nor appear in the advertising material or publicity connected therewith.
b) The design of the voucher or receipt used in such scheme, and the wording thereon, shall not be a colourable imitation of the general design and wording of the cards issued by Book Tokens Ltd.

20 Interpretation of these rules

All persons or companies selling or exchanging Book Tokens agree to do so in accordance with the foregoing rules 1–19 and the explanatory notes subjoined, and in the event of any dispute to accept the Directors decision as final.

Appendix 5

Net Book Agreement 1957 Standard Conditions of Sale of Net Books

(i) Except as provided in clauses (ii) to (iv) hereof, and except as we may otherwise direct, net books shall not be sold or offered for sale, or caused or permitted to be sold or offered for sale to the public at less than the net published price.

(ii) A net book may be sold or offered for sale to the public at less than the net published price if:
   (a) it has been held in stock by the bookseller for a period of more than twelve months from the date of the latest purchase by him of any copy thereof, and
   (b) it has been offered to the publisher at cost price or at the proposed reduced price, whichever shall be the lower, and such offer has been refused by the publisher.

(iii) A net book may be sold or offered for sale to the public at less than the net published price if it is second-hand and six months have elapsed since its date of publication.

(iv) A net book may be sold at a discount to such libraries, book agents (including Service Unit libraries), quantity buyers and institutions as are from time to time authorised by the Council of The Publishers Association of such amount, and on such conditions as are laid down in the instrument of authorisation. Such amount and conditions shall not initially be less or less favourable than those prevailing at the date of this Agreement.

(v) For the purpose of clause (i) hereof, a book shall be considered as sold at less than the net published price if the bookseller:
   (a) offers or gives any consideration in cash to any purchaser except under licence from the Council of The Publishers Association, or
   (b) offers or gives any consideration in kind (e.g. card indexing,

stamping, reinforced bindings, etc., at less than the actual cost thereof to the bookseller).

(vi) For the purpose of this Agreement and of these Standard Conditions:

Net book shall mean a book, pamphlet, map or other similar printed matter published at a net price. *Net price* and *net published price* shall mean the price fixed from time to time, by the publisher below which the net book shall not be sold to the public.

Public shall be deemed to include schools, libraries, institutions and other non-trading bodies.

Person shall include any company, firm, corporation, club, institution, organisation, association or other body.

(vii) The above conditions shall apply to all sales executed in the United Kingdom and the Republic of Ireland whether effected by wholesaler or retailer when the publisher's immediate trade customer, whether wholesaler or retailer, or the wholesaler's immediate trade customer, is in the United Kingdom or the Republic of Ireland.

Appendix 6

Library Licence

Terms and conditions

This Licence is issued by authority of the Council of The Publishers Association in accordance with Condition (iv) of the Standard Conditions of Sale of Net Books set out in the Net Book Agreement, 1957, to permit the Bookseller named overleaf ('the Bookseller') to supply the library named overleaf ('the Library') with net books, solely for the use of the library but not for resale, at a discount not exceeding ten per cent of their net published prices, subject to the following conditions:

1 Discount on net books may be allowed only in return for prompt settlement of invoices.
2 Discount may not be allowed on net books on which the Bookseller receives a discount of less than sixteen and two thirds per cent plus five per cent.
3 Discount may be allowed only so long as the Library's total annual purchase of net books solely for the use of the Library is not less than £100.
4 No consideration in cash or in kind, other than the granting of a discount permitted under this Licence, shall be offered or given by the Bookseller or sought or accepted by the Library in respect of, or in connection with, the supply of net books by the Bookseller to the Library.
5 Without prejudice to the generality of the last foregoing Condition, supplementary services (such as card-indexing, stamping, reinforcement of binding, the supply and fitting of plastic jackets etc.), if provided by or on behalf of the Bookseller to the Library, shall be charged and paid for at not less than the actual cost thereof to the Bookseller.
6 Books purchased under this Licence shall be purchased solely for the use of the Library and not for resale.
7 This Licence is revocable by the Council of The Publishers Association at any time but, unless revoked on account of a breach of the Standard

Conditions of Sale referred to above, not less than three months previous notice shall be given.

Any breach of these terms and conditions constitutes a breach of the Standard Conditions of Sale of Net Books referred to above and will render this Licence liable to immediate revocation.
Issued by:
The Publishers Association
19 Bedford Square, London WC1B 3HJ.
C. Bradley, Secretary & Chief Excecutive
For and behalf of
the Council

NOTE: This licence is valid only in respect of the Bookseller and the Library named overleaf and subject to the endorsement of their names being authorised by signature on behalf of The Publishers Association.

Text of Application for a Library Licence

To be sent to:
The Secretary,
The Publishers Association,
19 Bedford Square,
London WC1B 3HJ.

Application is hereby made on behalf of the library named below for the bookseller(s) named below (whose willingness to supply has been ascertained) to be licensed to supply the said library with net books solely for the use of the library (but not for resale) at a discount not exceeding ten per cent of their net published prices in accordance with the terms and conditions of the Library Licence set out overleaf.
The following undertakings are given on behalf of the applicant(s):

1 That current total annual expenditure on new net books for use in the Library is not less than £100 and that future expenditure on such books is expected to be about £ . . . *
2 That in support of the foregoing, the Library will on request provide The Publishers Association in confidence with particulars of the Library's annual expenditure on such books.
3 That the Library grants access† to the public free of charge and to this end undertakes that if a Licence is granted:
   (a) The applicant(s) will display in a prominent place outside the Library building and visible to the general public a notice stating that access to the Library is granted free of charge; and
   (b) The applicant(s) will use his (or their) best endeavours to procure the local public librarian to display in the local public library or libraries a notice to the public relating to the applicant's(s') Library, similar to that referred to in (a) above.
4 That if a Licence is granted, the applicant(s) will not seek nor know-

ingly accept any consideration in cash or in kind, in breach of the terms of the Licence, in respect of or in connection with the supply to the Library of net books.

5 That the applicant(s) understand(s) that discount may be allowed under the Licence only in return for prompt settlement of invoices, and that no discount may be allowed on net books on which the bookseller(s) receive a discount of less than sixteen and two-thirds per cent plus five per cent.

6 That the applicant(s) understand(s) that books purchased under the Licence must be purchased solely for the use of the Library and not for resale.

This application is made on behalf of the following library:
(Please give the full name and address)

The applicant(s) nominates for the said licence the following bookseller(s) whose willingness to supply has been ascertained. (Please give full names and addresses and attach a further sheet if necessary.)

*Please complete and attach any further information about the library (e.g. its date of foundation, specialisations, size of stock, etc.) which might assist the Committee charged to consider this application. A copy of your last Annual Report, for example, would be useful.

†For the purposes of the Library Licence the word 'access' shall be understood to mean (1) that the ordinary books in the libraries of the institutions concerned shall not be restricted to the use of the students or members of such institutional libraries, but (2) that under proper safeguards, and throughout the usual hours of such libraries, they shall be available, without charge, for public use within the library building. Satisfactory references or recommendations shall, where required, be submitted by strangers (as in the case of the British Museum) and discretionary power shall be vested in each library to withhold special works from general use, and to refuse to issue books to undesirable persons; but the free use of books shall not be unreasonably withheld.

Appendix 7

The Book Agent's Licence

The purpose of this Licence is to permit booksellers to supply net books at a discount to certain organisations which then sell them at the full published price. The organisations are usually churches, clubs and schools which are able actively to promote the sale of books, but which can only carry a small stock.

Book agencies in schools are granted only for the sale of net-priced recreational titles, and not for books destined for class or school library use.

Authorisation to supply net books at a discount to such organisations if given by the Publishers Association through the grant of a Book Agent's Licence. Some booksellers prefer to supply a stock of books to the school, which then sells them on their behalf, charging a commission for doing so. However, this is a less popular method than the Licence because the books remain the property of the bookseller until they are sold; if they become damaged or lost while at the school it is the bookseller who is out-of-pocket.

The organisation requiring a Licence must give, on an application form obtainable from The Publishers Association, the name of the bookseller(s) willing to supply under Agency conditions, together with an undertaking to sell net books at not less than their full published prices. The application must be accompanied by a registration fee.

Licences are granted by The Publishers Association.

The discount given by the bookseller to an agent must not exceed half that received as trade terms from the publisher.

Name
(If you have a business name, please show it)

Address

having applied for recognition as a Book Agent, and having given the undertaking printed on the back of this Licence, is hereby authorised to purchase new books: for resale to the public at the full published price, from the following bookseller, viz.,

these books being for recreational reading, entirely for resale at full published prices to individual purchasers (i.e. not for class or scholastic or library use) and the said bookseller is hereby authorised to allow the said book agent an allowance not exceeding fifty per centum of the retail discount given to the bookseller by the publisher in respect of each new book supplied to the book agent, BUT ONLY during the period for which this Licence is valid, and so long as the Licensee observes the conditions of his undertaking.

It is a condition of the granting of this Licence that it may be revoked at any time by the Publishers Association upon reason being given and upon its giving written notice by the hand of its Secretary to the parties named herein. But unless revoked on account of any action which the Publishers Association or the Joint Advisory Committee consider to be a breach of its terms and/or conditions three months' notice shall be given to the Licensee.

For and on behalf of
the Publisher Association

Secretary

Date of Issue

UNDERTAKING

This Licence is granted in consideration of an undertaking by the Licensee:

(i) not to offer for sale or to sell any new net book or books at less than the full net published price, either directly or indirectly or by way of settlement discount;
(ii) not to ask for or to accept any allowance upon new net books except from the Bookseller named upon this Licence or upon any endorsement thereof.

I/WE accept the terms and conditions of this Licence and undertake that they shall be observed in all dealings under its authority.

Signature of Licensee..

(in full) ....
Business name (if any)..
Business address..

Date ....

Appendix 8

Quantity Book Buying Scheme

(Revised (November 1954)

BEING A SCHEME DESIGNED TO EXTEND THE LARGE SCALE PURCHASE OF NET BOOKS BY INDUSTRIAL COMMERCIAL AND PHILANTHROPIC ENTERPRISES

1. The Quantity Book Buying Scheme, which was introduced by the Publishers Association and the Booksellers Association in 1937, was simplified in 1951 to provide for a discount to be given to those who *as an exceptional matter* ordered 12 or more copies of a title or titles, of which the total value was not less than £25. The scheme has now been amended and extended to cover large single orders for net books of an aggregate value of £250 or more, regardless of the number of copies of any one title contained in the order.
2. *Conditions of Licensing*

Licences for the grant of discount in accordance with the scale set out below will be issued by the Publishers Association under the Quantity Book Buying Scheme on the following conditions:-

(a) The books must be required for gift or presentation in connection with the purchaser's business, or for philanthropic or propaganda purposes. The provision of a library, whether recreational or educational, for use by the purchaser's own employees, free of charge, would qualify.

(b) The books are not to be offered for sale by the purchaser, nor is their use or distribution to be made subject by him to any charge or other consideration.

(c) The order will be delivered in one consignment and paid for in cash on receipt.

(d) No discount shall be allowable on books on which the bookseller himself does not receive from the publisher a discount of at least 25 per cent. The value of any such books shall be deducted from the total value of any order coming under this scheme before application is made for discount to be allowed.

(e) Licences issued by the Publishers Association under this scheme shall apply to one order only and shall not be valid for repeat orders (although application may be made for fresh licences in respect of repeat orders that qualify on their own account).

3. The scale of discount allowable shall be as follows:–

(*a*) *For an order for assorted titles worth £250 or more:*

Value of order	*Discount*
£250-£349	5%
£350-£449	6%
£450-£549	7%
£550-£649	8%
£650-£749	9%
£750-and over	10%

(*b*) *For an order for a large quantity of one title (minimum 12), to a total value of £25 or more:-*

A flat 10 per cent discount

Text of Application for a Quantity Book Buying Licence

Application for Licence for the Allowance of Discount

I/We (Name of Firm)..
of...
hereby apply for a licence to allow discount to:–
(Name of Customer)...
of...
in respect of an order for:

(Complete (*a*) for orders for assorted titles)
(*a*) New net books to the value of £...

(Complete (*b*) for orders for a quantity of one title.)
(*b*) copies of.. (title)
published by...
at (price)...
being fully satisfied that the books are required for purposes within the conditions set out overleaf, namely:–
....
....
(give details of exact purpose for which books are required) and that the purchaser understand and will comply with the said conditions.
Signed...
Date.......... Position in Firm..

For official use only.
To .... (booksellers)
of ....
You are hereby authorised to allow a discount of ....per cent to
....
on the above order
Signed...
Date .... Secretary, The Publishers Association

Appendix 9

Application for a Primary and Secondary School Licence

To: The Trade Executive
THE PUBLISHERS ASSOCIATION
19 Bedford Square, London WC1B 3HJ

Vat No: 233 577 359

We hereby apply for a Primary and Secondary School Licence. We have read the terms of such Licence and we agree to comply with those terms

Date:____________________

Name of organisation:____________________

Address:____________________

____

Telephone: ____________________

Name of Chief Education Officer/Head Teacher: ____________________

We certify that we are: *(Tick as appropriate.)*

(a) ☐ a primary and/or secondary school teaching a full curriculum to full-time students and accepted as such by the appropriate authorities:

(b) ☐ a local education authority (or government body performing similar functions) responsible for schools as defined in (a) above;

We buy books on a regular basis for the use of students in the school(s).

Our annual budget for such books is approximately: £ ________

In the case of (a):

The number of pupils in the school is: ____________

In the case of (b):

The number of schools for which we are responsible is: ________

and the total number of pupils in those schools is approximately:

____

We enclose our cheque for £23 (£20 plus VAT) for the administration charge.

Signed: ____

Name: ____________________ Position: ____________________

FOR OFFICE USE

Application received (date): ______________________________

Application checked and accepted (date and signature of person checking):

____

Licence despatched (date): ____________ Number of Licence: __________

Appendix 10

Book Agent's Licence (Services Unit Libraries)

Name of Unit

Address

having applied for recognition as a Book Agent in respect of a Unit Library, and having given the undertaking printed on the back of this Licence, is hereby authorised to purchase new books from the following booksellers, viz.:

and the said bookseller is hereby authorised to allow the said book agent an allowance not exceeding seven and a half (7½) per centum of the retail (published) price of each book supplied to the book agent, BUT ONLY during the period for which this Licence is valid, and so long as the Licensee observes the conditions of his undertaking.

It is a condition of the granting of this Licence that it may be revoked at any time by the Publishers Association upon reason being given and upon their giving written notice by the hand of their Secretary to the parties named herein. But unless revoked on account of any action which the Publishers Association consider to be a breach of its terms and/or conditions three months' notice shall be given to the Licensee.

For and on behalf of the Publishers Association

Date of Issue

UNDERTAKING

the Licence is granted in consideration of an undertaking by the Licensee:

(i) that the books bought under the authority of the licence will be used solely for the purpose of a Unit Library, will remain the property of the library and will not be resold except on the terms of the Net Book Agreement

(ii) that all orders for books bought under the authority of the licensee will be signed by a responsible Officer of the Unit

(iii) not to ask for or to accept any allowance other than that authorised by this licence and then only from the Bookseller named upon this licence or upon any endorsement thereof

I/WE accept the terms and conditions of this Licence and undertake that they shall be observed in all dealings under its authority

Authorised Officer ____________________

Unit ____________________

Address ____________________

____

____

Date ____________